"A relation[...] something that you need to work on frequently to keep it alive. The work that you put into it is like giving water to the plant so that it grows or like putting fuel into a car in order to run it on the road."

Dr. Sadhana Damani

Published by

Blue Stallion Pubications

(Part of The Oxford Development Centre)

The Oxford Development Centre
47 High Street
Witney
Oxfordshire
OX28 6JA

www.bluestallion.co.uk
www.oxdev.co.uk

Blue Stallion Publications is committed to
publishing high-quality therapeutic resource books
and works in close professional liasion with
The Oxford Stress and Trauma Centre.

Editor: Dr. Claudia Herbert
Cover and book design: Simon Ryder (www.artnucleus.org)
Photo: © iStockphoto.com/Dina Trifonova

ISBN 978-1-904127-08-6

Printed and bound in Europe

Resolving

Relationship
Difficulties

with CBT

Contents

Chapter Three: Assessing the situation

Chapter Four: Understanding filters, prickly thoughts and negative emotions

Chapter Five: How to use the worksheets to help you through the process

Chapter Six: Life practicalities

Chapter Seven: How to get the most out of your conversations with each other

Part II

Chapter Eight: Activities to enhance your well-being

Chapter Nine: Working through issues

Chapter Ten: The way forward

Appendices

Foreword

It has always been a surprise to me how little attention has been given by cognitive behaviour therapists in developing a better understanding of how people can be helped to work on overcoming relationship difficulties in the UK, compared to the USA, Australia and continental Europe.

Maybe relationship difficulties are not such a problem in the UK or maybe people muddle through "for better or for worse". This we know is just not the case and the breakdown in relationships is as much a problem here, as anywhere else in the world. We also know that the impact this has on many couples, and often on their wider family and friends, can be devastating.

Fortunately there are a number of excellent therapists and counsellors in the UK, as well as, organisations, such as Relate, that are aimed at helping people gain a better understanding of themselves and their relationship. However, there has been less available for people who want to try and work things out for themselves.

This book, the first in the *Resolving* series, fills that gap and provides a structured self-help guide that will help many couples identify, understand and begin to deal with their difficulties. It also introduces couples to cognitive behaviour therapy (CBT), which has been shown to be an effective therapy for helping people deal with a wide range of problems common in everyday life.

Sadhana Damani and Larissa Clay have produced a self-help guide, which is full of information about relationships and about using CBT to problem solve. It uses this information to explore the strengths people have, as well as, the ways of resolving the difficulties that all too often arise and place a strain on couples and, if not faced and dealt with, will end in a complete breakdown of the relationship. It further provides a clear set of practical and easy to follow exercises, which will help to develop the relationship and work through issues that couples may be facing.

The authors wrote at the beginning of the book that "A good relationship is about building a positive partnership and working together". This book will provide the basis for building and enhancing relationships or re-building relationships that have become difficult. I am sure it will be of benefit to many couples and individuals, as well as, being a very useful resource for those therapists and counselors who are working with couples facing relationship difficulties.

Rod Holland
British Association for Behavioural and Cognitive Psychotherapies (BABCP)

Part I

Introduction

The aims of this book

This book is written to help you to understand, identify and deal with some of the difficulties you may be experiencing within your relationship. Whether you feel the problems you face are small and manageable or quite overwhelming, this book will provide you with a number of tools, which others have found helpful in overcoming their difficulties. This book can be used independently at home by couples. If you feel that you need the help of a third party and you are thinking of or already have enlisted the help of a therapist or counsellor, this book might still be helpful as a useful background guide to Cognitive Behavioural Therapy (CBT) for your relationship difficulties. Your therapist or counsellor may also recommend using the exercises contained here to supplement your sessions.

We would like to mention at this point that this book is designed to be inclusive of all couple relationships between two adults. So, whether you are in a traditional marriage, in a single-sex relationship or co-habiting with your partner, whether your partnership is relatively new or of long-standing, we sincerely wish to help you overcome the difficulties you may be facing.

This book is divided into two parts. Part I introduces you to CBT and how it works. It takes you through various exercises on how to identify and resolve the difficulties you may be facing. Part II gives you suggestions and exercises to help you enhance your relationship. It also gives you information on how to work through specific issues you or your partner may be facing.

What is a good relationship?

First of all, what is a relationship? A relationship is a connection between two individuals and it can be positive or negative. A *good* relationship is one that is bonded by love, trust and commitment with a healthy measure of self-respect and respect for your partner. A good relationship also allows you to grow individually and, at the same time, to grow together in such a way as to make the relationship stronger.

It is one thing to *define* a good relationship, but what does this mean in practice? To put it simply, a good relationship involves more than being loving with each other and having good times together. It is also about having the *skills* to cope with times that are not so good.

Stephanie and Sam are a committed couple with two young children with all the normal stresses of family life. For eighteen months, they went through a very difficult time when Sam was made redundant. His loss of employment not only put a huge strain on their family's finances, but also affected his self-esteem. Stephanie had to work extra hours to help their family financially. However, Stephanie and Sam were able to get through this difficult time without any significant difficulties in their relationship and their family not only remained intact, but they were able to maintain their generally happy state.

When asked how they managed to cope, they said that they talked about everything – the situation, how they were feeling and where they thought they were headed. Although they did feel down sometimes, they always encouraged each other positively. When tempers rose through stress and fatigue they made a point of taking some time out from whatever they were arguing about so that the situation did not get worse. They also made detailed plans about how they would cope financially, until Sam found a new job. Sam himself made and acted on very specific plans about how he would find a new position. Each week they discussed these goals to see where they were going and kept each other up to date about any developments or changes that they needed to make.

We have probably all known people who, however bad the situation gets, are able to cope admirably with negative events. While it may seem like a natural talent for some people, for most of us, it requires some new learning. Stephanie and Sam not only recognized that they needed to *think* positively, they *behaved* in a positive and pro-active manner. In addition, they understood how to communicate effectively and set short- and long-term goals for themselves. Throughout all their difficult moments they were respectful of themselves and with each other. They understood how much they could handle under stress and took small steps to achieve their goals.

A relationship demands commitments from both parties to learn about each other and evolve together. A *good* relationship is about building a positive partnership and working together. The only way this can happen is through good communication. Later in the book we will talk about communication skills and how to express your positive and negative emotions, while remaining non-judgmental about each other.

Many things make a good relationship, but one very important factor that often gets overlooked is understanding what your life with each other means. Do you know what you and your partner want out of the relationship? Do you have specific mutual aims and goals for your relationship? Do you have a plan to make these things happen for yourselves? Do you assess your life together from time to time to understand what is happening in your relationship?

The above example with Stephanie and Sam shows how making specific plans and implementing certain actions to achieve your goals can help you as a couple to cope with a stressful situation. Moreover, it is the key to getting what you both want out of your relationship. Later in the book we will explain in greater detail how to use problem solving strategies and planning to enhance your life together.

You need to know what you want in order to make it happen and you need to be specific in order to communicate it to each other. Having clear ideas and a good joint understanding of what your life together is all about, is the core of a good relationship.

What are relationship difficulties?

Philip and Jemma love each other very much. They have a well-balanced life with many mutual interests and friends and they both work at careers they enjoy. However, from time to time they have disagreements that escalate into shouting matches that end with Philip storming out of the house and Jemma feeling tearful and angry. The next day, things return to 'normal', with nothing more being said about what occurred.

Perhaps you have experienced a similar scenario or know of someone who has. When asked about their relationship, Philip and Jemma said they felt their relationship was good generally, but that they were not very good at dealing with negative events in their life together. Jemma said she had been experiencing more anxiety lately and Philip said he had wanted to spend less time at home. One solution they had come up with was to try to avoid situations or conversations that could lead to disagreements. However, as we all know, it is simply not realistic to think we can control all the events in our lives. Furthermore, by not discussing them and, more importantly, *not learning how to deal with them,* these negative events were occurring with increasing frequency. This left both of them feeling that perhaps their relationship really was not as good as they had thought.

From time to time you may find yourself involved in arguments or feeling less than happy with yourself or with your partner. Perhaps domestic issues, such as dealing with finances or the lack of time in a busy life have resulted in feelings of stress or fatigue. These and other negative feelings and situations do not necessarily constitute relationship difficulties if you and your partner are able to deal with them effectively and resolve them in a satisfactory manner.

However, like in Philip and Jemma's case, difficulties arise when issues are not communicated or resolved in a way that is beneficial to the relationship. When this happens, negative emotions, such as, anxiety, depression, anger or grief can build up, which, in turn, can bring out all sorts of unwanted thoughts and behaviours.

These behaviours can range in severity from refusing to speak with each other to shouting matches. Using abusive language towards each other or feeling the lack of physical desire and intimacy for your partner for a prolonged period of time can be symptomatic of relationship difficulties.

How can you deal with these difficulties?

So, what can you do to deal with these unwanted behaviours? Usually, it is all too easy to see the symptoms or the behaviour that is hurting us. Even when we realize that certain behaviours are damaging the relationship, it may be difficult to understand how to make changes.

This book uses an approach based on Cognitive Behavioural Therapy (CBT) that couples can use to overcome the difficulties they may be experiencing in their relationship. We give you information on identifying what constitutes your beliefs about the relationship and how some of these thoughts may be the underlying cause of the problems that you are having.

The problem-solving strategies in this book can help you identify and deal with the current difficulties in your relationship. You will also find practical guidelines and exercises to help you and your partner work together to deal with day-to-day demands. Once learned, these skills can be used to cope with any future difficulties that may arise.

How to get the most out of this book?

Throughout the book we will give you various exercises to do on your own and with your partner. To get the most out of this book, we strongly recommend that you do these exercises. You can only discover aspects of your relationship, identify areas that need improvement and incorporate changes if you participate in this process. So, to this end, we encourage you to follow our suggestions and do the exercises in each chapter.

Writing things down

Writing things down will help you in many ways. There are very good reasons for doing this.

When you write things down, it helps you to remember what you want to do or say. We have all made a 'to do' list or a shopping list at some point in our lives to help us to remember what it is we need to do. It helps us to be more efficient and it lessens the chances of forgetting something important.

Writing things down helps us to organize our thoughts and behaviours. Let's look at the 'to do' list as an example. Initially, you may jot down five things you need to do that day. Then, when you look at it, you realize that if you do it in a certain order, it will save you time and effort. It is the same process when it comes to discussions. You may both have similar items that you wish to discuss, so writing them down may help you to organize your discussions and use your time more effectively. You can prioritize the issues and decide what areas need to be addressed first. You may find it helpful to number these issues in order of priority. If you find that two issues are of equal importance, try to resolve the easier issue first. This applies to all the items on your list. Starting with the easy issues first will strengthen your confidence in your ability to handle other issues from your list.

If you write down what you think or feel, it helps you to make it specific for yourself and for your partner. The more specific you can be, the better the chances of identifying what the real problems are. Writing also helps you to make your thoughts and feelings more concrete. In other words, it can help you to better understand what you think and feel about a particular situation.

Writing things down can help alleviate some of the stress you may feel, because it helps you to understand it better. When you feel less anxious, you will be able to relax more and be in a better frame of mind to discuss the problems you are facing.

Writing down what you discussed helps you to remember it in the future. Very few of us have perfect memories and even at the best of times, two people can remember the same event in different ways. Because of this, writing things down serves as a helpful record of what you discussed.

Finally, talking about the difficulties in your relationship can be very emotional. Writing things down before, during and after the discussion can help you to keep on track with your discussions and not become carried away by your emotions. You may also find that the collaborative nature of writing together about your discussions (and doing the worksheets later on in the book) can be an enormous step towards honest and effective communication, which, in turn, will help you to resolve the issues you are facing.

So, we cannot stress enough the importance of *writing things down*!

On a practical note

We suggest that you each get a blank notebook or a ring binder with blank pages for yourselves. Keep this handy so that you can jot down ideas as they come to you. Dedicate your notebook for this purpose and the exercises we recommend. Each partner should keep a notebook for themselves. As you proceed through each chapter, these notebooks will show you just how far you have progressed in building a better understanding of your relationship.

What is CBT?

CBT – Cognitive Behavioural Therapy

The approach we use in this book is based on Cognitive Behavioural Therapy (CBT). Cognitive refers to thoughts. What we think about a certain situation in our lives can produce either a positive or negative feeling and that can affect how we behave.

Our behaviour has a big impact on our daily lives. Positive emotion usually produces positive behaviour. For example, if you are happy – a positive emotion – you communicate this either verbally or non-verbally and others notice your happiness. If you have a negative emotion – you feel sad – you may cry or your facial expression may look more somber and your tone of voice may be less energetic. If you experience stress, you may become agitated, panicked or find that you cannot sit still.

The CBT* process helps you to identify the negative thoughts that produce the negative feelings that impact on your behaviour and the way you see yourself and the world around you. CBT then teaches you how to modify these thoughts, so that they have a much more positive impact. Essentially, this process can help you

---

*CBT or Cognitive Behavioural Therapy is actually the integration of two cognitive and behavioural therapies. Many clinicians and scientists have contributed to this sophisticated and effective therapy. In the 1950s, Dr Albert Ellis developed Rational Emotive Behavioural Therapy (REBT). In 1965, Dr Aaron T. Beck applied cognitive therapy to depression and found it to be a very useful therapy. CBT is a good evidence based therapy and it is recommended in the UK by the NICE (National Institute for Health and Clinical Excellence) to treat many simple to complex problems.

work through whatever thoughts, emotions, bodily feelings and behaviours and their subsequent actions may be hindering you from experiencing the positive aspects of your life together.

Automatic and 'prickly' thoughts

Sometimes, thoughts can become so fixed in our minds that they become automatic. You can become so conditioned to thinking automatically about certain events that you are not truly seeing the event for what it is. We call these thoughts *'prickly'*, because in most cases, they are negative thoughts that leave us feeling distressed, sad or very negative.

Here is a common example of automatic, prickly thinking:

David is a good cook. One day he made a birthday cake for his partner, but the cake did not turn out exactly as he had anticipated. He started to think that he was not a good cook at all and told himself that he was useless. Before long he had convinced himself that he had never been a good cook and that he should never try making anything again.

This line of thought can have a negative impact that goes far beyond one slightly less than perfect birthday cake. Despite the fact that he had had many successful results in the past, David's thoughts about his abilities went from bad to worse and that affected his mood. Although his partner was sincerely delighted that David had made a cake, David's perception of himself and his failures resulted in a discouraging atmosphere and their time together was not very celebratory.

Perhaps you can see that if David had been able to follow a different line of thought, his feelings about himself and, ultimately, the success of the birthday celebrations would have been much different. That is where CBT can help.

Let's see how it works

We have adapted Dr Aaron Beck's CBT model for this book. What do we mean by 'model'? Think of the model as a sort of map or outline that shows three processes that operate most of the time: what we think, what we feel and what we do.

We have designed three simple models to show you how this works. The first model illustrates the individual's process. The second model shows the process within the couple's relationship and how it impacts on each person and the relationship as a whole. The third model shows what happens when you work together to resolve the issues you have been experiencing.

Here is summary of the terms we use in this book:

EVENT – what has happened.

FILTERS – our assumptions about ourselves and others. This refers to our mindset through which we interpret events.

THOUGHTS – what we think about the event.

FEELINGS – how we feel (good, bad, positive, negative).

EMOTIONS – the emotions we feel (angry, sad, happy, hopeful).

BEHAVIOURS – how we act, based on how we feel.

MODEL ONE – Understanding the event

Model One shows the processes that we all go through. In the first instance, we experience an **event.** We then process this event through our **filters**. These filters are not actual physical parts in our body, but refer to the assumptions that we make, based on what we have experienced in the past. We interpret the event accordingly and we think about it. These **thoughts** influence how

Model One

THE EVENT
What's happened?

How we BEHAVE,
based on how we feel
and what we think

OUR FILTERS
How we interpret
the event

How we FEEL
about the
event

What we THINK
about the event

we **feel** about the event and what **emotions** we experience. Depending on how we feel about it, we **behave** in particular ways, which will differ from each other one way or another.

MODEL TWO – Understanding the event within the couple's relationship

Model Two (*see next page*) illustrates a common scenario in which couples find themselves. Each person in the relationship experiences the same **event**. However, each person reacts differently, depending on what **filters** they have. One or both partners make assumptions about themselves and their partner.

When you make assumptions about your partner, you actually think that you know what they are thinking or what they will say without having a discussion about it. These assumptions also influence how you interpret the event and what thoughts and feelings you have about it.

Relying on assumptions often produces those **prickly thoughts** we discussed earlier, which can result in **feeling** low or negative. These thoughts and feelings influence what we say or how we **behave**. If you are feeling negative, you will probably end up reacting in a negative way. This reaction compounds the problem and prevents you from dealing with the original event effectively.

MODEL THREE – Re-interpreting and moving on from the event

Model Three (*see next page*) highlights the need to explore the **event** together. It shows that good **communication** and

Model Two

Partner A & Partner B
THE EVENT
What's
happened?

Partner A
MY FILTERS
How I interpret
the event

Partner B
MY FILTERS
How I interpret
the event

What I THINK
about the event

What I THINK
about the event

How I FEEL about
the event. What
are my emotions?

How I FEEL about
the event. What
are my emotions?

How I BEHAVE,
based on how I feel
and what I think

How I BEHAVE,
based on how I feel
and what I think

What IMPACT did
our actions have on
our relationship?

Model Three

Mr & Mrs A
THE EVENT
What's happened?

Mr A
MY FILTERS
How I interpret
the event

What IMPACT did our
actions have on our
relationship?

Mrs A
MY FILTERS
How I interpret
the event

How we BEHAVE,
based on how we feel
and what we think

Communicate
& negotiate use
WORKSHEETS 1, 2, 3

How we FEEL.
What are our
emotions?

Mr & Mrs A
OUR FILTERS
How we interpret the
event

What we THINK
about the event

negotiation are the key to this process and how participating in it can affect each person's filters and their responses – thoughts, feelings, and behaviour – to the event.

Talking about the event and what you think and feel about it, helps you to understand each other's filters. It also gives you insight into the way your partner thinks. The more you do this, the more you will come to understand how and why each of you reacts in the way you do. At first, many couples are surprised by how differently each partner responds to the same event. Going through this process will help each partner to identify and modify their specific filters, – the assumptions that are contributing to the conflict in your relationship. As you learn more about each other you will form new filters together as a couple – **our filters** – which will help you interpret the event rationally and respond to each other appropriately.

To help you to communicate and negotiate effectively we have designed a set of worksheets, which we talk about in *Chapter Five – How to use the worksheets to help you through the process*. We will also introduce you to John and Tara, who use the worksheets to move forward in their relationship.

How this approach can help you

Models One, Two and Three show the interrelationship between your thoughts, feelings, emotions and behaviours. These are the factors that influence the quality of your life as individuals and as a couple, from how you deal with practical issues, such as running your household, to your emotional and physical well-being.

This CBT-based approach can help you to focus on identifying and resolving your difficulties. In the next chapter, we will show you how this process works in practice.

As you use this approach, you will probably find that your discussions will become more structured and effective.

It can help you to explore the difficulties you are experiencing in a time-limited format so they do not drag on for too long and exhaust everyone in the process. This active, problem-solving based approach can help you to achieve real results. The collaborative nature of the process can help to strengthen your ability to work together and bring about a positive effect on your relationship.

Other factors

We have spent some time discussing how our thought processes can have a positive or negative impact on our lives and relationships. Please remember, too, that there are many external factors that influence your relationship: your environment, your job, your children, your health, your extended family, etc..

For example, the main source of the problem you are facing may be environmental. Perhaps your living environment is less than ideal for you and your family and this is resulting in high levels of stress. You may decide that you cannot change the source of the problem, but you might still be able to better manage its effects on your relationship by using some of the skills that you can learn here.

While it is important to consider how these other factors affect you and your relationship, do try to keep your focus on using the CBT approach to improve on those aspects that can be in your control, such as the nature of the interactions within your relationship.

The science bit

Recent medical studies have shown that various chemicals in the brain play a role in our moods. When these chemicals are in balance, we feel better. Making changes in our lifestyle has been shown to affect the balance of these chemicals. In *Chapter Eight – Activities to enhance your well-being*, we discuss how a proper diet, exercise and enough sleep can help keep these chemicals in balance and provide you with a solid foundation for a good, healthy life.

Assessing the situation

Before you explore the difficulties you are having in your relationship, it is helpful to assess the current situation of your life together. What are the strengths in your relationship? What opportunities are there to enhance your relationship? What are the obstacles you face? Identifying the strengths and opportunities will give you a positive platform on which to base your discussions about the problems you are experiencing.

It may be tempting to skip straight to the sections dealing with the obstacles in your relationship or the problem-solving solutions we suggest. We urge you strongly to do each exercise in order, because it will give you a far stronger platform from which to deal with any issues you may have in your relationship. We also present these exercises again in *Appendix Five* as a quick reference and so that you may photocopy them if you wish. Keep focused on each exercise and be specific. And, as we recommended in *Chapter One – Introduction*, do write your thoughts down in your notebooks!

Identifying your strengths

For many of us, it is all too easy to list our faults or think negatively about ourselves and our abilities. Likewise, it is often easier to think about everything that is wrong with our partner and the relationship than it is to acknowledge the positive qualities. While it is important to be realistic about ourselves and our relationship, it is much easier to resolve problems if you start together from a position of strength. In this section, we would like you to identify your strengths and positive qualities as individuals and as a couple within your relationship.

EXERCISE ONE – Identifying the strengths

An exercise sheet can be downloaded from: www. oxdev.co.uk or see p.188

As your first exercise, write down a list of your strengths as an individual. Each person should do this on their own. Strengths can be skills, abilities, a talent or simply what it is you feel you are good at. Here are some examples:

> *I am a good listener.*
> *I am organized.*
> *I am creative.*
> *I am a caring person.*
> *I am enthusiastic.*
> *I am calm.*

Next, write down a list of what you see as your partner's strengths. As with identifying your own strengths, think about your partner's talents, abilities and what you see as their good qualities. Here is a short list to get you started. My partner is...

> *patient*
> *affectionate*
> *reliable*
> *good with people*
> *attentive*

Finally, write down a list of what you see as the strengths of being together as a couple. Again, write these down on your own without conferring with each other. Think about the positive aspects of being together. Here are some examples:

> *We make time to do things together.*
> *We share household chores.*
> *We have similar interests.*
> *We make a good team.*
> *We help each other.*
> *We make each other laugh.*
> *We enjoy good physical contact with each other.*

If you are not used to thinking about yourselves in a positive light, this is an excellent opportunity to look at yourselves in a new way. Make the list as personal and detailed as you like. If you find it difficult to get started, ask someone their opinion. Try asking different people in your life, for example, members of your family, your close friends or your colleagues.

You may feel less than positive at the moment, but try to think about the qualities that you bring into the relationship that enhances it and then think about what your partner brings, even if you feel that these qualities have not been in evidence for a long time. Think back to a time when they were a part of your lives together. You may like to add to this list over time as you discover new strengths about yourselves.

Once you have written down your strengths as an individual and as a couple, it may be helpful to come together and talk about what each of you has identified. You may be pleasantly surprised at what the other person has written! Please do not be judgmental or upset, if your lists differ. Most people see themselves and their relationships in their own unique way. Keep in mind that this exercise is designed to enhance how you see yourselves and each other.

This exercise will also help you to validate your strengths as an individual and together as a couple. By all means remember to refer to this list and remind yourselves of the positive qualities when you are facing challenges within your relationship.

Identifying the opportunities

Once you have identified and explored your strengths, use them to do something that will enhance your relationship. These are what we call the opportunities that exist in your relationship. Take a look at the opportunities present within your relationship. Do this as a joint venture. For example, if you both like spending time with each other, create a special time to be together. If you share similar interests, perhaps you can participate in some activity together. For example, if you both enjoy cooking (a strength) you might decide to cook a meal together. Some opportunities are spontaneous. Let's say you may both enjoy going to the cinema. You suddenly find yourselves free from your usual commitments one afternoon so you decide to go see a film together even though it is out of your usual routine.

Opportunities are whatever helps your relationship work better and brings you closer together. The ideal situation is when each partner plays to their strengths in the relationship and, as a result, each partner feels better in themselves and also feels that the partnership is enhanced.

EXERCISE TWO – Identifying our opportunities

An exercise sheet can be downloaded from: www. oxdev.co.uk or see p.188

For your second exercise, write down what you think are the opportunities present in your relationship. Again, do this individually and then come together to talk about what each of you have identified.

It may help you to start by looking at what you identified as your strengths of being together as a couple. Here are some examples of strengths and their opportunities.

STRENGTH	OPPORTUNITY
We both have an interest in art.	Let's take a painting class or visit a museum or the art gallery together.
We both enjoy physical contact with each other.	Let's plan an evening at home alone.
We're each good at different tasks and chores around the house.	Let's decide who does what, so our household runs more efficiently and each person feels well supported.

Once you start to identify the opportunities present in your relationship, you may find there are many more than you may have considered at first. Choose one or two that you can do easily and be specific about what you will do and then see it through.

By identifying the opportunities that are already present in your relationship and building on them, you strengthen your experience together as a couple. The more you do this, the more it will help you when you need to deal with the difficulties you may be experiencing in other areas of your relationship. Even if you are not currently facing problems, it is still helpful to be aware of the opportunities that exist, so that you can ensure that you are making the most of them.

Identifying the obstacles

Now that you have identified your individual strengths, your strengths as a couple and the opportunities present in your relationship, you may see that you have quite a lot going for you. What is holding you back from fulfilling your potential for a full and happy life together?

If you are having problems in your relationship, most likely you have some obstacle, which is hindering you from fulfilling your needs as individuals and as a couple. It is helpful to identify the obstacles you are facing and what the underlying problems are so that you can be mindful of them.

EXERCISE THREE – Identifying our obstacles

An exercise sheet can be downloaded from: www. oxdev.co.uk or see p.188

As with the previous two exercises, write down what you feel are the obstacles in your relationship. Do this individually before coming together to have a talk about it.

Obstacles can be emotional or practical. For example,

you may feel frustrated much of the time. You may also feel that the frustration is stopping you from getting the best out of yourself and the relationship. Or, you may feel that your partner is not at home enough and that it is affecting your family life. Below are some common obstacles faced by many couples.

> *We never have time to be alone together except to sleep.*
> *The house is such a mess I can't think of doing anything else.*
> *I'm too tired to do anything in the evenings.*
> *My partner doesn't listen to me.*
> *We never have the money to do the things we want.*
> *I can't make plans for us as a family, because my partner is unreliable.*
> *I don't know how to talk about what I feel.*
> *We argue over how to raise the children.*
> *Problems don't get resolved. We fight a lot.*
> *Our relationship lacks intimacy.*

Some (or all) of the above obstacles may sound familiar to you. Once you have each written down and tried to clarify for yourselves what you feel the obstacles are in your relationship, come together to discuss what you have both written.

Please remember to give each other equal time to express each other's thoughts. This is the time to get ideas into the open, so it is especially important to refrain from arguing or making judgments about what the other person is saying. Keep this initial session short. Try to have this discussion when you are not too tired and when you know you will not be interrupted by other people. Most importantly, please do not become disheartened if you find that there are difficult issues that need to be addressed. You have just made an important first step in acknowledging that they exist.

At this point, you may find it useful to read *Chapter Seven – How to get the most out of your discussions*. It contains guidelines on how to communicate more effectively. This may be especially useful if this last exercise generates material that is emotionally painful. Do also read the section entitled *Establishing your coping point* in the same chapter, since this will help you become aware of your stress levels and what to do about it.

You may find it very difficult to face some of the problems that exist in your relationship. Staying calm and being respectful of each other is even more important when emotions are running high. Agree to talk about one issue per discussion and to take a short break to bring stress levels down before continuing. In these cases, it is usually better to have short discussions. Agree to spend thirty minutes at the most and refrain from talking about it throughout the rest of the day.

This exercise could potentially generate material that is emotionally very painful for one or both of the people in the partnership. If you feel that it is something with which you cannot help each other, we suggest that you contact your GP to get some professional help. If you feel that you can help each other with the issue, then we strongly advise you to follow the suggestions in the following chapters about being mindful about how you are feeling and how you can help each other by communicating, listening and being nonjudgmental. We have discussed these topics in Chapters Seven, Eight and Nine.

Making time to relax and reflecting on what you have learned and how you can help yourself and your partner is also very helpful. We acknowledge how difficult it can be to face some of the problems that may exist in your relationship. One partner may also feel stronger about one problem than the other and this is important to acknowledge. You may also have different levels of ability in dealing with the difficult issues as they emerge. If you feel that you have identified this as a strength, then you can use it and cope with the emotions and feelings as they surface. However, it is important for you to know your 'coping point' and the 'cut-off point' as explained in Chapter Seven. Please make sure that you read and understand this. This will help you not to burden each other with extreme emotions and feelings. It is essential that this exercise becomes an opportunity rather than another obstacle so that you can feel that there is scope to make positive changes together in your relationship.

Once you know what you need to work on, you can prioritize your problems. This way, you will be able to use your time effectively and not feel overwhelmed by having to deal with too many issues at once.

EXERCISE FOUR– Prioritizing our list

An exercise sheet can be downloaded from: www. oxdev.co.uk or see p.188

If you find it difficult to decide what problem holds the greatest priority, write down all the problems or issues that you have both identified into one single list.

Next, separate the items on this list into two lists, putting the items of greater priority into the first list (List A) and the items that can be left to be discussed later in the second list (List B).

Once you have two separate lists, do the same again with the items in List A. Continue to do this until you have identified the one or two key issues that you both feel need to be addressed first.

If, at any point, you cannot agree on what items should go into List A, each person can try to identify what they consider to be the one or two most important issues and put them into List A. From this list, see if you can agree to prioritize the issues in it for discussion. Sometimes it is much easier to agree on what needs to be talked about first, if there are only a few items on the list. You can try putting rating or a percentage next to each item and take the easiest one to tackle first. This way you will be able to prioritize and feel good about achieving the task, as well.

If you still cannot agree on which topic ought to be discussed first, each person should put what they consider to be the most important topic in List A. Once there are only two items in this list, toss a coin to determine which topic will be discussed first.

Once the topic for discussion has been selected, focus on it and give it your full attention, even if it was not your choice of topic. Keep it fair: take it in turns to decide what topic will be discussed. This way, each person's concerns are validated, which makes you more receptive to working together.

Asking for help

As you work through the obstacles you face in your relationship, it is important to be mindful about your needs as individuals and as a couple.

If you feel you need help and you feel that your partner can give you the support and help you need, then ask them for help.

If either of you ever feel that you need help from a professional, you can contact your doctor for assistance. They can refer you to a suitable professional in your local services. You can self-refer to some of the services, especially private psychotherapy or psychology services. Some details of useful addresses are given at the end of this book. If you want to see a professional privately, you can contact organizations, such as, BABCP, which is The British Association of Behavioural and Cognitive Psychotherapy or UKCP, which is The United Kingdom Council for Psychotherapy, for details of Accredited Cognitive Behavioural Psychotherapists.

Even if it has been a very long time since both you and your partner have worked together in a constructive manner, showing respect and concern for each other's well-being is a positive affirmation of your commitment to each other. Allow and enable yourselves to make this process as positive and constructive as you can. The more supportive you can be of each other, the greater the chances that you can find solutions to tackle your problems together.

chapter four

Understanding filters, prickly thoughts & negative emotions

So, what causes the negative behaviours in a relationship? The key to this answer may lie in what you or your partner believe about yourselves and the relationship.

Filters in the relationship

First, we will explain what filters are and how they impact on our lives. Filters are assumptions, a type of deep, underlying thought, that most of us have about ourselves and the world around us. These thoughts may often be based on what we have experienced. For example, we 'assume' it will rain, if the sky looks dark and cloudy or we 'know' that the traffic will be heavy at certain times of the day, because these are things we have experienced repeatedly. Most of us are fairly flexible about these kinds of assumptions. It might not rain despite the dark clouds or the traffic may be unusually light, in which case we accept the fact that the reality was different from our assumptions and carry on with our day.

Assumptions may also act as a filter through which we interpret what happens to us. It is similar to wearing glasses. If the glasses are clear and in focus we can see clearly. However, if the glasses are out of focus we may not be seeing the true picture. In fact, we may *believe* we see one thing, when in fact, something else has occurred.

Difficulties with assumptions arise when we insist that our assumptions are always correct. We might not recognize the possibility that our assumptions may be hindering us from understanding a situation clearly. Can you imagine what your day might be like if you could not accept that the reality was different from your assumptions? Using the example of the weather, if there are dark clouds in the sky, you might assume that it will rain. If it does rain, your assumptions are correct. However, let's say it does not rain. Instead of simply accepting that your assumptions were not correct on this occasion, you insist that it should rain or even act as though it is raining. If this is how your mind operated, you might find yourself confused at the very least.

Sometimes, we have assumptions about ourselves and our partners. We use these assumptions as a filter to interpret an event. Often, however, it may not be an accurate interpretation of what really happened. When we use assumptions to interpret an event, it can produce prickly thoughts, negative emotions and feelings. As a result, this can have a negative impact on the relationship.

Here is an example of how this works. One day, your partner suddenly asks you to stay at home to wait for a delivery. You cannot do this, because you have made commitments about helping at a school function. Imagine that you believe that being a good partner means that you are always available for your partner. Because you believe that you should always be available for partner, you might start thinking prickly thoughts, such as, *"I'm not a good enough partner."* Next, you might start feeling guilty about letting your partner down and feel increasingly bad about yourself, all because you were unable to fulfill your assumptions about yourself.

This assumption could also work against your partner. Let's say that it was you who asked your partner to suddenly stay at home and they were unable to do so. Because your partner did not fulfill the assumptions you have about people in relationships, you start thinking prickly thoughts, such as, *"My partner doesn't care about me enough."* Next thing you know, you may feel resentful towards your partner or feel sorry for yourself. In either case, it is unhelpful for the relationship if you go about thinking and feeling this way.

When we make assumptions about our partners, we believe that we know what they are thinking or what they will say. This situation frequently leads to avoidance. We do not bother to ask questions and explore our partner's actual thoughts, feelings or intentions, because we think we know what the other will say or do. When we feel anxious about exploring our partner's thoughts, feelings or intentions, we are more likely to avoid discussion and leave things unspoken. We may not even realize that we are feeling anxious.

Unfortunately, leaving things unspoken usually leads to more anxiety and an even greater desire to avoid discussing it. This produces a pattern of spiraling anxiety and avoidance becomes the accepted manner of dealing with the difficult issues, or rather, not dealing with those issues!

Identifying filters and beliefs

We often have to do some work to understand our own individual filters. What are our filters and how do they affect how we interpret an event? If we can understand what these filters are, we can then see how they may be affecting not only ourselves, but the way we interact with our partner.

EXERCISE FIVE – Identifying our filters and beliefs

An exercise sheet can be downloaded from: www. oxdev.co.uk or see p.188

Write down what you feel are some of your filters about your relationship. The following is a selection of assumptions and beliefs commonly held by many people about their relationships. Do you find that you are holding any of these assumptions?

If my partner loves me or cares for me then he/she:

> *will not argue with me*
> *will not hurt my feelings*
> *will show me love*
> *will not get angry*
> *will agree with me on whatever I say*
> *will not make me feel upset*
> *will not have problems in the relationship*
> *will always know what I am feeling without my having to explain it*
> *will not interrupt me*
> *will always be interested in whatever I am talking about*
> *will always spend a lot of time with me*
> *will want sex to the same degree as me*
> *will always know what I want without my having to ask for it*

Now, take some time to identify your underlying beliefs about yourself and write them down. Here are some examples to get you started. To be a good partner/to be loved, I should:

> *never argue*

> *never have or show negative feelings*

> *not get angry*

> *not feel upset*

> *not have problems in the relationship*

> *always earn plenty of money*

> *always have plenty of time for everyone*

> *always put aside my interests for my partner*

> *always want sex to the same degree as my partner*

> *always be the one to look after the children*

> *always keep the house perfect*

> *always be happy*

A good relationship is one where:

> *we never fight*

> *we never argue*

> *we always want the same things*

> *we always agree*

> *we always want to do the same things*

> *we always have plenty of money*

> *we always have plenty of time*

> *we never lose patience*

> *we always want intimacy, physical contact, sex at the same time*

> *we are interested in the same things*

> *we like the same food, books, films, activities*

> *we never have to have difficult discussions*

> *we always want to be together*

These assumptions are just a selection of those which you may hold about yourself and others. Once you begin to explore your own beliefs, you will most probably discover your own set of assumptions through which you filter events.

Identifying the prickly thoughts

Once you identify the assumptions you have about yourself, your partner and your relationship, you will be able to identify the thoughts that are related to that particular event. Make a list of these prickly thoughts, especially the ones that make you feel sad or angry. Most certainly, these thoughts are having a negative effect on your relationship.

EXERCISE SIX – Identifying my prickly thoughts

An exercise sheet can be downloaded from: www. oxdev.co.uk or see p.188

Write down what you think are some of the prickly thoughts you have had about yourself, your partner or your relationship. It may be helpful to think of a recent event when you felt some negative emotions and then try to identify some of the thoughts you had at that time. Here are some typical prickly thoughts you may have had about yourself:

> *I'm not good enough*
> *I'm too good for him*
> *I'm stupid*
> *I'm being taken for granted*

Perhaps you will recognize some prickly thoughts you have had about your partner:

> *He doesn't love me.*
> *She doesn't care for me.*
> *He's judging me.*
> *She doesn't try hard enough.*
> *She doesn't find me as attractive as the person she's talking to.*
> *He'd rather be with someone else.*
> *She's going to leave me.*
> *He never notices me.*
> *She doesn't appreciate me.*
> *He's selfish.*
> *She's stupid.*

And finally, you may have had prickly thoughts about your relationship:

> *This relationship is too much hard work.*
> *Our relationship is dull.*
> *This relationship isn't going anywhere.*

Remember, the prickly thoughts listed here are simply an example. You may recognize some of them as similar to yours or you may have a completely different set of prickly thoughts.

Sometimes assumptions and prickly thoughts can appear to be the same thing. It might be helpful to look at assumptions as something you generally believe and the prickly thought as something that can upset you. For example, you might believe that your partner should be able to know what you want without you having to tell them. That is your assumption and chances are, you will soon find that your partner will not be able to meet this expectation, since it is unrealistic for one person to be able to read another person's mind. When your expectation is not met, you might find yourself thinking thoughts, such as, *"My partner doesn't love me or care for me,"* or, *"My partner is ignorant"*. These are prickly thoughts, because they will most likely cause you to feel negative emotions: you may feel rejected or resentful. Whatever the negative emotion, it causes you to feel unhappy and upset.

Understanding negative emotions

In order to identify your prickly thoughts and the emotions they produce, it is helpful to understand negative emotions. Most of the time negative emotions are easy to identify in that they cause you to feel upset. The main negative emotions are feelings of sadness, anger and fear. However, negative emotions may sometimes be more subtle so that it takes some practice in order to identify them. The following are some of the ways these three main emotions might be expressed.

Sadness can manifest as feelings of:

> *alienation*
> *isolation*
> *depression*

> *disappointment*

> *insecurity*

> *hopelessness*

> *unhappiness*

> *rejection*

Anger might be behind feelings of:

> *frustration*

> *destructive tendencies*

> *jealousy*

> *hatred*

> *loathing*

> *fury*

> *envy*

> *spite*

> *bitterness*

> *resentment*

Fear can take many forms:

> *anxiety*

> *distress*

> *nervousness*

> *panic*

> *feeling overwhelmed*

> *worry*

> *uneasiness*

> *dread*

EXERCISE SEVEN – Identifying my negative emotions

An exercise sheet can be downloaded from: www. oxdev.co.uk or see p.188

Once you identify some of the prickly thoughts you have, write down the negative emotion you feel that goes along with that thought. For example, if you write, *"He doesn't find me attractive"*, the accompanying emotion or emotions might be insecurity and jealousy. If you write, *"She's lazy"*, the emotion might be sadness, feeling overwhelmed, bitter or worried. Sometimes it can be difficult to identify how you feel or have felt in a given circumstance. Write down as many thoughts and emotions about it as you can. You may then find that some of the feelings are stronger than others.

Sometimes it may be difficult to acknowledge that you feel certain negative emotions at all. For example, you might discover that you feel resentful towards your partner or your children for demanding so much time from you. It is not uncommon then to feel guilty for feeling this way. Unfortunately, feeling guilty does not help you to resolve your initial negative emotions. Instead, it helps you to avoid them. So, if you find yourself feeling guilty for feeling negative emotions, write it down and acknowledge that you feel this way. This is the first step towards understanding what is causing the negative emotions and resolving them. Often, especially with guilt, there is another, deeper underlying emotion, which is covered by the guilt. Through acknowledging your guilt, you may be able to recognize the co-existing, deeper emotion. This can be any emotion, as mentioned, above.

What are you getting out of your assumptions and prickly thoughts?

For the final section in this chapter we would like you to consider what you get out of believing your assumptions and thinking the negative prickly thoughts. It might surprise you to think that you are getting something out of believing and thinking anything negative. However, it is not necessarily anything positive that you are getting out of thinking in a negative way. Imagine that you believe you are incompetent at cooking. Each time you try to cook you think prickly thoughts like, "*I'm not a good cook. I have no confidence at cooking*". As we explained above, you will then probably have negative emotions due to your prickly thoughts. Now ask yourself, what are you getting out of believing this about yourself and thinking this way? Your immediate answer might be, "*nothing*", because you can see no advantage or positive gain, and you would be right if we were only talking about advantages and positive gains. Now, think about the disadvantages of thinking this way. One clear disadvantage is that this kind of thinking is probably causing you to feel unhappy about this aspect of yourself. What you also get out of thinking this way is that it '*allows*' you to stay incompetent. Instead of being proactive and doing something positive so that you feel you are a better cook, this thought keeps you from moving forward.

As you become more aware of the advantages and disadvantages of your beliefs and prickly thoughts, you will most likely see that there are few positive advantages to thinking negatively.

An exercise sheet can be downloaded from: www. oxdev.co.uk or see p.188

EXERCISE EIGHT – Identifying what I am getting out of my filters and prickly thoughts

Go through your previous notes on your assumptions and prickly thoughts. Choose one or two beliefs or thoughts, write them down and ask yourself what you get out of believing this assumption or thinking these prickly thoughts. Write down what you think are the advantages of thinking this way and the disadvantages of thinking this way. How does this assumption or prickly thought cause you to behave? Does it make you act in a positive, proactive manner or does it make you act in a negative way? Does it actually stop you from acting or doing anything at all? By asking yourself these kinds of questions, you will be able to see whether you are getting positive gains from your beliefs and thoughts or if they are actually preventing you from getting the positive gains that would help you to feel happier in yourself.

The reason we ask you to do the exercises in this chapter is, because they will help you to become used to identifying what you are thinking and feeling. It might seem odd to have to think about and identify what you think and feel and you might be saying to yourself, *"But of course, I know what I think and feel!"* We have tried to show you in this chapter that sometimes the things we believe (our assumptions) and the prickly thoughts we have, are so ingrained in our thinking that they are automatic. Prickly thoughts in particular can become habit forming so that you are not consciously aware of thinking them until you stop and try to identify them.

In the next chapter, we will explain how to use the worksheets and take you through an illustration of a couple, who have used them to resolve some of their issues.

How to use the worksheets to help you through the process

In the first part of this chapter, we will show you how to use the worksheets to identify and resolve some of the problems or issues you may be experiencing in your relationship. Later on, we will guide you through an example of how one couple, John and Tara, use the worksheets to work on the problems they are experiencing in their relationship in order to move forward.

We have created a set of three worksheets to use at different stages as you explore the issues in your relationship. In the following section, we explain step-by-step how to fill out these worksheets. If you are already familiar with this kind of activity, you may feel that this section is a little self-explanatory, in which case you may wish to skip ahead to the section on John and Tara. However, it may still be helpful to read this section on the worksheets, since it includes suggestions that may help you identify and understand your situation more clearly.

You may already have a good idea of what you feel you need to talk about – perhaps you are experiencing increasing conflicts over practical concerns like money, or maybe you feel that you are growing apart from each other and that is the cause of the strain on your relationship.

Don't worry, however, if you feel you are not sure as to where to start. It is not uncommon to experience problems within a relationship and yet not be able to pinpoint the underlying cause of it. These worksheets are designed to help you explore together various events and your feelings surrounding them, which, in turn, can help you understand better what may be the source of your difficulties.

The worksheets

We have created a set of three worksheets for you to use to help you through the process of identifying your difficulties and working to resolve them.

As you may recall, in *Chapter Two – What is CBT?* the models showed you how we experience an event and then, consequently, how we have thoughts and feelings about it. In the previous chapter, *Chapter Four – Understanding filters, prickly thoughts and negative emotions* we talked about the prickly thoughts that you might find yourselves thinking concerning the event and the negative emotions you may feel as a result of this pattern of thinking.

WORKSHEET ONE – Understanding what happened

The first worksheet, *Worksheet One – Understanding what happened* is designed to help you identify the event and your thoughts and emotions surrounding it.

A worksheet can be downloaded from: www. oxdev.co.uk or see p.183

Each partner should fill out their own *Worksheet One* so that you are able to record how you each perceived what happened. Do this worksheet independently of each other.

Fill out your name at the top of the worksheet. Write down the event that you wish to talk about in the first column.

You may find yourselves wondering what constitutes an 'event'. Think of it as something about which you find you are having prickly thoughts and negative emotions. It may be something obvious, like a disagreement that escalated into a fight that left you feeling angry, hurt or bewildered or the event may be something more subtle and cumulative. Perhaps you feel your partner is taking you for granted, because of a series of little things they have assumed you will do or that as a couple, you do not manage practical aspects of your life together very well and this is causing conflict. You may find your reactions are becoming stronger or that you are feeling increasingly unhappy about a situation. Either way, an event in this context is something that is affecting you and your relationship in a negative way.

Write down everything you think might be the event. Don't worry about 'right' and 'wrong' answers – simply write down how you see the event. If you feel the event itself is overwhelming in its scope, break it down into several small events to help yourselves understand it better. For example, in the first instance, you might write that you and your partner had a fight about the children. Once you give it some thought, you will most likely be able to break this down into further detail: you argued over who does more in terms of taking care of them; how one partner seems to have to impose all the discipline; how the one partner seems to take for granted that the other partner will deal with certain issues; or how one partner makes decisions without consulting the other, etc. If you can break down a big event into smaller, more specific events, it can help you to identify the thoughts and feelings you had about them, which can also help you to identify the underlying issues that may be the cause of the problem.

In the second column, write down your **prickly thoughts**. If you have more than one prickly thought about the event, write them down in the same column.

In the third column, write down your **emotions and feelings**, which you experienced as a result of the event and the prickly thoughts you had about it.

In the fourth column, give each of the emotions and feelings you wrote down in the previous column a **rating**. Use a scale of 1 to 100, with '1' being the mildest and '100' the most intense feeling.

In the fifth column, write down **what you would like to change**. This change is something that you would like to do or that you want your partner to do to help to resolve the situation. If what you write in this section involves your partner participating in or doing something different from you, write down specifically what it is that you want them to do. You can also include an idea of the timeframe in which you wish to make these changes.

Doing *Worksheet One – Understanding what happened* will help you to identify your thoughts and emotions surrounding the event. In the next section, you will use this information to talk with each other about what happened. You will each have the opportunity to talk about what you thought and felt. This process can also help you to start to identify some of your assumptions, which may be contributing to the negative situation. Once you have both had the opportunity to talk about the event, you can start to talk about how to change the situation.

WORKSHEET TWO – What we are going to do

A worksheet can be downloaded from: www. oxdev.co.uk or see p.183

The purpose of *Worksheet Two – What we are going to do* is to allow you to bring your ideas together with regards to what you want to change and how to go about making those changes in your lives together.

Now that you have both had a chance to reflect on and write about the event that you found problematic in *Worksheet One – Understanding the event,* use these worksheets to facilitate a talk about what you need to do to help resolve the problems you have identified.

It would be helpful for both of you to sit down and fill this worksheet out together as you discuss the event.

Write down what you have both agreed on as the **event** that prompted this discussion. This event is the same one that you identified in *Worksheet One.*

Fill in each partner's name. In the box underneath each name, each partner can sum up what they thought or how they felt about the event.

The next section, **discuss together**, is essentially the action plan you create together to help resolve your issues. Use what you have written in Worksheet One to help you to discuss and then agree on what changes you wish to make. Write these down under what we **want to change.** You may wish to number them according to priority.

Next, talk about what you both need to do in order to bring about these changes. Write these down under **what we are going to do**. You may also wish to talk about a time frame for the activities you write down in this section. While some of these may be daily actions, it may be helpful to agree that certain things will be done by a certain date. Make sure that these changes will help both of you to achieve what you set out to achieve. Once you start realizing these goals for yourselves, you will start to feel more positive about your relationship.

Please remember to use good communication and negotiating skills through your discussions with each other. Always remain non-judgmental about what the other person suggests so that you both remain calm and open to new ideas and ways of doing things.

In the final section of this worksheet, **set a date** to do *Worksheet Three – Where we are now,* draw up a timeframe for your action plan. For example, you may decide to do *Worksheet Three* in one month's time. Use the space in this section to make a note of any topics you might like to discuss at that time.

You may also find it helpful to include a review date when you will sit down and discuss how the plan is progressing. The review date can be independent of the dates in your time frame. Try to schedule regular and frequent review dates to help keep you on track. This will help you to bring up any problems you may be having in completing a task, but also, it will provide you with an excellent opportunity to communicate with each other about the successes you are experiencing.

Once you put into practice your action plan, you will most likely feel less distressed and more relaxed, because you are taking positive action to resolve your issues.

WORKSHEET THREE – Where we are now

This worksheet is for each partner to evaluate their thoughts and feelings about their current situation for a period of time, as decided on *Worksheet Two – what we are going to do.* Once you have each had time to reflect on your progress, you can use this information to give each other feedback and have a talk about where you feel you are in your relationship.

Fill in your name at the top of the worksheet. Each partner should do this worksheet independently of each other. If, however, you find it difficult to do so on your own, you can write down your thoughts while you talk about it together. Each person should still fill out their own worksheet, since the information is personal to each individual.

Write down the **date**. This is helpful, especially if you decide to do these worksheets from time to time to evaluate your progress. This way, you have a record of your thoughts and feelings and how you viewed your relationship at certain intervals.

For the first column, **what are my thoughts now?**, write about what you have been able to accomplish individually and together as a couple.

In the next column, **how do I feel now?**, write down what your feelings are currently about the original event.

In the third column, **emotions and feelings**, make a note of your current emotions and feelings.

In the fourth column, **rating**, give each of your emotions and feelings that you listed in the previous column a rating. Use a scale of 1 to 100, with '1' being the mildest and '100' the most intense feeling.

The last section on this worksheet is entitled, **how much the event has been resolved? Is there any further action required?** Write down what you think is the current situation. If the situation has improved or been resolved, think about whether there are any changes that you will have to commit to, or continue to act on, in order to maintain progress.

If the event has not been resolved, this is an excellent opportunity to talk about what you feel has been successful, what actions may not have been as helpful as expected and what changes still need to be made to make more progress. You may feel it is helpful at this point to work through another *Worksheet Two* to set out another action plan.

We hope that you, as a couple, will benefit from working with these worksheets in order to be able to identify the ways in which you can be the most supportive toward each other. The process of working through the worksheets, participating in creating an action plan and taking positive steps towards resolving your issues will help you to replace your existing filters and thoughts with more constructive beliefs and thoughts about yourselves and your relationship. When you begin working together with the new knowledge and skills you gain, you will find it can help you to let go of your old filters and thoughts. As you gain a new understanding of yourselves, you will find you develop filters as a couple and that you work better together as a team.

To give you an understanding of how you can use the worksheets to identify and work to resolve the issues in your relationship, we would like to introduce you to John and Tara.

John and Tara

John and Tara have a good relationship and they have been married for three years. However, they have experienced some difficulties with John's sudden bursts of temper. In all other respects, John and Tara communicate well, but she has noticed that John refuses to acknowledge having negative feelings, especially anger, when they attempt to discuss it. Without warning, John will explode, shouting and saying hurtful things. Tara loves John and feels he is a good partner, but his unpredictable bursts of anger leave her feeling uncertain. John usually calms down within an hour and is very apologetic. Tara feels he is genuinely sorry for his actions, but she does not understand why he reacts in such an angry manner. John and Tara decided to work through this issue following a similar episode. John had lost his temper when he could not get the computer to work.

The next day, when he had calmed down, they worked through *Worksheet One – Understanding what happened* and *Worksheet Two – What we are going to do* to help them understand the event, how they felt about it, what they wanted to do to and how to bring about the changes they wanted.

John (*see opposite*) wrote down what he regarded as the event from his point of view and then noted his prickly thoughts about it. Now, take a look at Tara's worksheet (*see p62*).

As you can see, her perception of the event is a little different from John's. John's understanding of the event has to do with his feelings about not being able to get the computer to work, while Tara's view of the event is about the impact John's burst of temper and his behaviour had on her.

Although they are not the same version of the event, neither person is "wrong". They simply see and experience it in different ways. Likewise, the prickly thoughts they think and the emotions they feel are not exactly the same. What is similar, however, is

WORKSHEET ONE
UNDERSTANDING WHAT HAPPENED

NAME	John
EVENT	Yesterday evening, I couldn't get the computer to work. I got angry and then got angry with Tara and said hurtful things to her.
PRICKLY THOUGHTS	I feel that I am not a good husband because of the way I react to situations.

EMOTIONS & FEELINGS	Sad	Frustrated	Scary
RATING	95%	100%	90%

WHAT I WANT TO CHANGE	I want to stop this happening.

WORKSHEET ONE
UNDERSTANDING WHAT HAPPENED

NAME	*Tara*
EVENT	*John's sudden burst of temper last evening. He refuses to acknowledge having negative feelings. John shouts and says hurtful things.*
PRICKLY THOUGHTS	*I hate this in John*

EMOTIONS & FEELINGS	*Sad*	*Stressed*	*Hurt*	*Trust*
RATING	*90%*	*95%*	*95%*	*15%*

WHAT I WANT TO CHANGE	*I need to discuss this with John and need to do sometihng about this within a week or so.*

that both John and Tara recognize that they want something to change. Already, they can identify that there is an opportunity in this situation. Neither feels okay with this state of affairs or the fact that it seems to recur and they both want to do something about it.

After they completed the first worksheet, they came together and had several conversations about what they had written. They talked about the event itself, how they felt and what they felt the impact was on them.

By working through *Worksheet Two – What we are going to do (see pp64–5)* they came to some decisions about what it was they wanted to change and what they would do to work towards those changes. They felt it was important to try to understand each other's feelings, but also for John to learn better ways to express his feelings. He decided to learn and try to practise some relaxation techniques so that he could calm himself down when he felt overwhelmed by his temper.

John and Tara also practiced improving their communication skills. Tara asked John how he was feeling in a quiet, non-threatening way and John tried to express his feelings honestly in a calm voice, using 'I' statements.

By working through these worksheets and discussing together the discoveries that he had made, John was able to identify his filters involving anger, which in turn, was affecting his behaviour. He realized that he felt frightened whenever he felt anger, and that caused him to pretend he was not feeling this emotion.

Where do these filters come from? Sometimes, our beliefs are formed very early in our childhood. They are our attempt to make sense of ourselves, other people and the world around us.

For example, as a young child, John's parents shouted and

WORKSHEET TWO
WHAT WE ARE GOING TO DO

EVENT	Sudden burst of temper yesterday evening	
NAME	John	Tara
	I don't understand why Tara wants to understand how I feel. I don't really understand how I behave is upsetting to her.	I want John to understand that I hate it when he has a sudden burst of temper.
WHAT WE WANT TO CHANGE	(1) understand each other's feelings (2) identify whatever it is (his assumptions) that triggers John's behaviour (3) how John expresses his feelings; John's behaviour (4) what to do under the circumstances and for John to be aware of it (5) to discuss how to help ourselves to relax and think about alternatives to deal with the prickly thoughts	

WORKSHEET TWO
(CONT.)

WHAT WE ARE GOING TO DO

(1) John will tell Tara when something is upsetting him
(2) to be aware and be mindful about the discussion, use the alternatives and to relax.
(3) John to relax with Tara's help in the beginning and Tara to support John
(4) John needs to remember to start to use the alternative ways to express his thoughts and feelings and make notes if needed to remind himself.
(5) to give constructive feedback to each other without being judgemental

SET A DATE TO DO WORKSHEET THREE – WHERE WE ARE NOW

(1) how John is doing in verbalising how he feels – (in one month – 30th October)
(2) how Tara feels aout the alternative ways John is using (in one month, 30th October)
(3) how both of us feel as a couple about this and what needs doing next

punished him every time he tried to express feelings of anger. Instead of being taught how to communicate anger in an appropriate manner, he learned that expressing anger was a scary experience and that it was safer not to express it at all.

Consequently, he assumed that anger was a bad emotion and that people who cared for each other would never feel anger towards each other. This assumption made relationships very difficult for him. If his partner Tara ever expressed anger, he was shocked and hurt by it. He could not believe she could love him if she was angry with him. In turn, when John felt anger, he felt very guilty about it. Furthermore, because of his beliefs, John could not tell Tara he was angry. He would simply pretend he did not feel it, even if she asked him how he was feeling. His anger and frustration would build until it exploded in a rage, which would leave Tara feeling bewildered and hurt.

John's belief that it is scary to express anger and that bad things happen to him when he does helped to form his filters that people in relationships should not feel anger towards each other. However, it is unrealistic to expect people to not feel emotions, so this expectation caused problems for John and Tara. John's unpredictable and explosive expression of pent-up anger was also damaging Tara's trust in John.

The foregoing section about John's childhood is included to show the connection, in his case, between his early life experiences and his current filters. Please understand, however, that it is not necessary to always identify the source of your filters. It can be enough to recognize that you may hold certain negative assumptions and beliefs in order to see how they may be affecting you and your relationship. While John was able to see that his assumptions were related to his childhood experiences, the most important discovery for him was to identify his assumptions about anger and the feelings he associated with it. Once he had done so he could start working on his filters and learn to recognize them when they arose.

It is not uncommon for unrealistic filters and prickly thoughts to go hand in hand. When we or our partner cannot live up to those expectations, negative thoughts are often the result, which then cause the negative emotions that we feel. The best way to counteract the prickly thoughts is through repeated positive reinforcement of a different reality. In John's case, he assumed that it was wrong to feel angry in a relationship, whic, of course, is totally unrealistic. Every time he experienced anger with Tara, his negative thought pattern kicked in, which resulted in explosive anger. This reaction helped to confirm his filters that anger was something very scary. Once he had identified and understood his filters, he could counteract his prickly thoughts with positive experiences. With Tara's help, he came to understand that anger could be expressed in a safe, calm and accepting manner.

Prickly thoughts and negative emotions and feelings can come about for all sorts of reasons. The important thing is to understand the beliefs, which are causing them and try to counteract them in a practical manner together. Tara was not only interested in helping John, but she also participated actively to help him come to a new understanding of how to express negative emotions, in this case, anger. For many couples, much of the stress in the relationship stems from their filters – the assumptions they have about how the relationship should function.

After the first month, John and Tara reviewed their situation by

working through *Worksheet Three – Where we are now*.
John (*see pp69–70*) came to replace his initial belief (that expressing anger was a scary experience) with an alternate belief, that it was okay to feel anger and that it was permissible to express it appropriately. Communicating his feelings in a calm manner made it a safe experience.

As part of this process, it was also important that Tara (*see p71–2*) listened to John and they then discussed ways to resolve whatever was causing the anger.

As you can see from these last two worksheets, Tara and John felt much more positive about their relationship after engaging in their action plan, than they had at the beginning of this process. Although, in this instance, the problems they faced stemmed from John's filters as an individual and his ensuing behaviour, they both discovered things about themselves once they embarked on their action plan. Most significantly, both partners had to be equally committed in trying to resolve this issue. By doing so, they came to a much improved understanding of themselves and their relationship. Once they had completed all three worksheets, they compared their initial rating of their emotions and feelings in *Worksheet One* to their present rating in *Worksheet Three*. They discovered that there was a significant difference and that overall, they both felt sixty to sixty-five percent better than before.

As a result of this process John and Tara managed to understand what helped them to move on from the event. The following diagrams (*see pp73–4*) of *Model Two* and *Model Three* illustrate John and Tara's thinking immediately following the event and after they thought about it and talked about it.

WORKSHEET THREE
WHERE WE ARE NOW

NAME	John
DATE	30th October
WHAT ARE MY THOUGHTS NOW?	I think that I have more understanding of my angry outbursts and how it affects Tara and our relationship. I have learnt to recognise this and what to do about it. I have learnt to communicate my feelings of anger in an appropriate manner and most importantly, I have learnt to express it rather than bottle it up.
HOW DO I FEEL NOW?	I feel that I can talk to Tara about how I feel and that she supports me. It is not as scary as it used to be and I feel more relaxed in myself.
EMOTIONS & FEELINGS	A bit more relaxed. Happier in myself.
RATING	60% 65%

WORKSHEET THREE
(CONT.)

HOW MUCH THE EVENT HAS BEEN RESOLVED?

My difficulties with feeling and expressing anger are not resolved completely, but I have started to work on it more each day. I have also started to appreciate Tara's patience with me. I would say that this event is resolved approximately 40-45%.

IS THERE ANY FURTHER ACTION REQUIRED?

My commitment to maintain this progress: I acknowledge that I need to relax more, listen to what Tara and I discuss together, and to talk about my needs and our needs as a couple. I will continue to work on these areas. I need to continue to be an effective communicator and I feel that we need to do this Review Worksheet in one month. (30th November)

WORKSHEET THREE
WHERE WE ARE NOW

NAME	*Tara*
DATE	*30th October*
WHAT ARE MY THOUGHTS NOW?	*John and I have managed to discuss the issues together and it has made our relationship more relaxed as a result. I am no longer constantly on edge, wondering when John will get angry and start shouting.*
HOW DO I FEEL NOW?	*I listen, support and help John to express his feelings and he has started to do it by himself to some extent as well. So, I feel that as a result, our relationship is much more relaxed and it feels calmer than before.*
EMOTIONS & FEELINGS	*Relaxed* *Happier* *Hopeful*
RATING	*50%* *70%* *50%*

WORKSHEET THREE
(CONT.)

HOW MUCH THE EVENT HAS BEEN RESOLVED?

I feel that it has been resolved to some extent approximately 50%.

IS THERE ANY FURTHER ACTION REQUIRED?

My commitment to maintain progress is to be an effective communicator. I will be mindful about my emotions and needs. I will help John in such a way that he starts to chill out more and we start to celebrate our progress. We need to perhaps review this again in one month. (30th November)

Model Two: John & Tara

John & Tara
EVENT WHAT'S HAPPENED?
John's sudden burst
of temper

John
MY FILTERS
If people are for each other then
they should never feel anger towards
one another; therefore, I should
never feel angry towards Tara.

Tara
MY FILTERS
If I say or ask anything
John will feel angry as he
has done before.

What I THINK about the event.
I cannot tell Tara that I feel
angry. I need to pretend that I
do not feel angry.

*What I THINK
about the event.*
Why does John not
talk about it.

How I FEEL about the event.
What are my emotions?
I feel frustrated, anxious
and I feel low.

How I FEEL about the event.
What are my emotions?
I feel hurt, scared and
bewildered.

*How I BEHAVE, based on how I
feel and what I think.*
I behave very differently when
I'm angry. I explode, shout,
say hurtful things and become
agitated.

*How I BEHAVE, based on how
I feel and what I think.*
I avoid trying to talk about
it or resolve it and become
withdrawn.

*What IMPACT did our actions
have on the original event?*
The whole atmosphere becomes sad and
we avoid each other and as a result our
relationship becomes sour.

Model Three: John & Tara

John & Tara
THE EVENT
John's sudden burst
of temper

*What IMPACT did our
actions have on our
relationship?*
Things feel better now
and we feel a little more
reassured about the future.

Tara
MY FILTERS
It is okay to talk
about how you
feel.

John
MY FILTERS
If I talk about how
I feel then it might
be a problem.

*How we BEHAVE,
based on how we feel
and what we think*
Our life together feels more
relaxed, because there is a lot
less exploding and shouting.
We are not avoiding the
issues anymore, so we do not
feel withdrawn or agitated.

*Communicate
& negotiate use*
WORKSHEETS 1, 2, 3

John & Tara
OUR FILTERS
(1) it feels better to communicate how we
feel and what we can do to help; (2) it is
okay to feel anger and it is permissable to
express it and communicate it; (3) this helps
both of us to express how we feel and helps
us to understand the event better.

*How we FEEL.
What are our emotions?*
It feels much more comforting
and relaxed than before, as
we have come to a common
understanding.

What we THINK about the event
It is good that we have started to sort things out. We
can tell each other how we feel and why we do what
we do so that we can help each other.

Model Two shows that John and Tara had very different filters through which they perceived and thought about the event. While they both felt negative emotions, John tended to feel frustrated, while Tara felt hurt and bewildered.

As you can see in *Model Three*, however, John and Tara managed to re-interpret and move on from the event. They used the worksheets to talk about what they thought and how they felt. They negotiated over what they needed to do in order to have a positive outcome. They developed their own set of filters ('our filters'), which they worked out by using the worksheets. These joint filters also gave them the common foundation they needed to start to work on their issues. They started to feel relaxed with each other as they gained a shared understanding of each other's emotions and feelings. As a result, they felt closer and more confident about talking to each other about how they felt. John and Tara came to realize that their decision to work on their issues and take positive action as a response to the original event led them to a deeper understanding of each other and enhanced their relationship.

chapter six

Life practicalities

Learning to manage our life and primary relationship is a real skill. In *Chapter Three – Assessing the Situation*, we asked you to assess the current situation of your life together. In the section on *Identifying the opportunities*, we asked you to explore what you would like to see happening in your life. In this chapter, we will encourage you to expand on this by taking a look at where you are, what your life together is all about and where you would like to go in practical terms.

What do we mean by life practicalities?

Life practicalities are all the practical aspects of your life. How much income do you have and how do you spend it? How do you get to and from work? Who picks up the children from school and who looks after them? Where do you go on holiday and for how long? How is the weekly shopping organized and how are the various roles and tasks in your partnership distributed? Most of the above life practicalities are probably familiar to you, but you may also have some additional ones not mentioned here that you would like to add to your personal list.

Why do we need to think about life practicalities?

It is important to consider your life practicalities, because they affect how you feel about yourself, your partner and your relationship. For example, if you both agree on how the household bills get paid and each person keeps their part of the agreement, that part of your life will run smoothly and you will feel positive about it.

If you can identify and understand what your life practicalities are, you can plan for them better and avoid having those prickly thoughts we talked about in Chapter Two. Imagine the following scenario where you and your partner have never talked about money and agreed on how it is spent. One day, you may find yourself thinking that your partner is spending more money than you and conclude that this means that your partner is selfish. Or perhaps you have not agreed on who does what with regards to driving the children to their various activities. You might think that you do the entire running around and end up feeling resentful towards your partner. These kinds of prickly thoughts produce negative emotions and feelings, which in turn, affect your relationship.

The best way to pre-empt these prickly thoughts is to identify your life practicalities and explore and agree with each other how you will manage them. When each person understands his or her respective responsibilities in the relationship and delivers on what has been agreed, life can run a little more smoothly. Usually, it helps partners to feel not only happier, but also more secure and satisfied in their relationship. Furthermore, it strengthens your confidence in each other and brings you closer together, as you experience how successfully you can work together as a team.

Assessing your life practicalities

It is useful to assess your life practicalities from time to time, especially during times of change in your life. For example, when your children start school the way in which you manage your day will most likely change. Likewise, when you retire from work your daily routine will change. If your income rises or falls it is important to consider what changes you may need or want to make in your everyday life, as well as, in your long-term plans.

EXERCISE NINE – Exploring our life practicalities

An exercise sheet can be downloaded from: www. oxdev.co.uk or see p.188

For this exercise, write down what you consider to be your life practicalities. Here are some examples, but most likely you will find many more that are personal to your life.

> *Work*
> *Money*
> *Starting a family*
> *Holidays*
> *Chores around the house*
> *Being able to spend more time at home*
> *Caring for an elderly parent*
> *Planning for retirement*
> *Returning to education*

You can do this exercise on your own or together, but it may be helpful at first to think about it on your own, so that each person has a chance to come up with their own perspective. Then, you may like to set aside some time to sit together and explore with each other what all your current life practicalities are. Go through your lists and put them together. When you have written them all down, evaluate what you think is working well and how both of you feel about these aspects of your lives. Then, consider which areas need more of your attention and where you think changes maybe necessary. For example, you may find that you are happy about the way you and your partner manage money on a day-to-day basis, but you want to be able to save more money in the longer term. Or perhaps you want to move to a smaller house or a different location, because your children have left home.

Once you identify the practical issues that you think need to be addressed, you can explore with each other the changes you will need to make in order to achieve the result you would like to see.

Establishing your aims

Whether you have been together for many years or are just embarking on a relationship with each other, it is important to discuss your aims. In the beginning, you may only have been aware of falling in love and wanting to spend the rest of your lives together. At some point, however, the practical demands of daily life will catch up and then have to be met. Planning for a family and one's financial future; how to fit careers around a relationship; where to go on a holiday and how to budget for it, are just some of the decisions most couples will face. Having common aims in your relationship can strengthen the bond between the two of you and allow you to build up confidence in each other as you work together toward fulfilling your aims.

EXERCISE TEN – Establishing our aims

In the previous exercise, you were asked to explore your life

An exercise sheet can be downloaded from: www. oxdev.co.uk or see p.188

practicalities. You may have identified areas in your life that you wish to change or act upon. For example, let's say you identified that your house was too small for your family or that communication between the two of you was not as effective as it could be. Your aim, then, might be to build an extension to your house or to improve your communication techniques.

In this exercise, write down what you wish to achieve at this point in your life. If you are having difficulty getting started, think about something that you would like to work towards. Again, you can do this on your own at first and then come together to talk about it.

Remember, aims may be emotional, physical and/or practical. For example, your aim can be to spend more intimate time together; this could be seen as an emotional aim, because you want to feel closer to your partner. However, developing intimacy may involve practical aims as well, like making more time to spend together. Your aim may be to organize your finances, so that you have greater financial security, which is both an emotional and practical aim. Or perhaps your aim might be that you want to make changes in your lifestyle, so that you and your partner can become more healthy and less stressed. This could be both a physical and emotional aim. The more you understand what you and your partner want, the more you will also understand each other's behaviours, thoughts, emotions and feelings. When you feel that you have a shared understanding of your aims as a couple, write them down so that you can access them at later dates.

Revisit your aims from time to time. Your aims and your commitment to them may change as your relationship with each other evolves. Once you have achieved certain aims, others may come along to replace them. Make a written note of these changes and your new shared aims.

Setting your goals with the 'EARTHS' checklist

Once you have established and agreed on the aims in your relationship, think about what you and your partner may have to do in order to go about achieving them. These will be your goals that help you to fulfill your aims. We will show you how to set up a specific action plan in the next section, but at this point, it is important to get a more specific understanding of what might be involved in order for you to achieve each aim.

When setting your goals, you may find it helpful to apply the 'EARTHS' checklist to them. 'EARTHS' is an acronym for the basic elements to consider when setting your goals. You want to ensure that your goals are effective, achievable, reasonable, thoughtful, helpful and specific.

'E' – Being effective

It is important that you think about each and every step, what the tasks involve and the time frame within which you want to complete them.

'A' – Achievable goals

Once you identify the goals you feel will help fulfill your aims, look at them and decide whether you need to break them down into little goals so that they become more achievable. This is important, because when you achieve your goals, it helps you to feel more positive as you move closer to fulfilling your aim. In turn, you will gain more confidence to work towards achieving the rest of your goals; even the ones that looked difficult at first will seem easier to achieve.

'R' – Reasonable goals

Your goal needs to be reasonable. Your expectations of what you can do, who can do what and within what timescale needs to be realistic so that you can reach to your destination in a reasonable manner. When your goals are reasonable, you will have a much higher rate of success in achieving them.

'T' – Thoughtfulness

Being thoughtful is the most essential element in this process of goal setting. Be aware of what you and your partner can and cannot do. Remember not to be judgmental and always look at the strengths and the skills that each one has so that they may be used effectively.

'H' – Being Helpful

When you are discussing and deciding on your goals and putting together your action plans, try and be helpful by working together without being judgmental or argumentative. Try to be flexible and open to suggestion.

'S' – Being specific

Be specific when agreeing on your goals. Decide on long-term, medium-term and short term plans. Short-term plans are probably those that can be accomplished from week to week or month-to-month. Medium-term plans are usually anywhere from six to ten or twelve months. Long-term plans can vary from one to two or up to five years. You can decide on the length of time for yourselves and what you feel is appropriate to your goals.

EXERCISE ELEVEN – Setting our goals

An exercise sheet can be downloaded from: www. oxdev.co.uk or see p.188

As with previous exercises, you may find it helpful and more time-efficient to first think on your own and then come together to discuss this. Go through your list of aims and talk about them. Think about what you will need to do, both individually and as a couple, in order to carry them out. If you have a long list of aims then think about prioritizing them. If you need help doing so, we explain how to do this later in this chapter.

Use the EARTHS checklist to help yourselves define goals that are manageable and effective. Talk about the strategies that you would like to use for some of your goals.

Once you have agreed on the basic goals write these down.

Now that you have agreed on the fundamental goals, decide on a realistic timeframe in which to achieve them and then write this down.

If you have little experience of goal setting, it may be helpful to start with an aim that is relatively easy to accomplish.

Writing an action plan

An action plan is basically your strategy for fulfilling your aims and goals. Let's use the example of buying a house to demonstrate how it works. Imagine that you decide that you want to be able to purchase a house in two years' time. You will need to go over your monthly income and outgoings and decide how you can budget yourselves in order to save a certain amount of money every month to reach your goal. The action plan helps you to define who does what or what you wish to achieve by a certain date and the steps you will take to accomplish your goals. When you have a specific action plan, each person knows exactly what the goals are and what they need to do by a certain time.

EXERCISE TWELVE – Writing our action plan

An exercise sheet can be downloaded from: www. oxdev.co.uk or see p.188

To write an action plan, you need to plan together how you will go about achieving the goal. Consider ways in which the goal can be achieved and agree on who will do what.

Once you have your main goal, timeframe and an understanding of what needs to be done in order to achieve that goal, you have your action plan. Now break down your overall goal into smaller goals, both in terms of the tasks involved and the timeframe. This will make it more manageable and allow for more flexibility, if required.

For example, imagine your long-term goal is to save a certain amount of money over two years. You agree on a budget, which might involve cutting down on certain expenditures and working more hours to generate more income. You might then choose to break down this two-year action plan into a shorter, monthly one, where you have a savings goal for each month. You may decide that saving the same sum every month works well for you. On the other hand, you may find that you can save more in some months than in others, in which case, you can work those fluctuations into your overall plan.

Breaking the action plan down into a monthly plan also means that the tasks (and target times) for which each partner has responsibility can be discussed and agreed upon in greater detail so each person knows what they are doing and feels supported in their efforts. As you meet your short-term targets, you will most likely find yourselves feeling positive about working together towards your common goals. This, in turn, acts to strengthen your commitment to your overall aims within your relationship.

Goal setting can be helpful in achieving emotional, as well as, practical aims and objectives. Perhaps you wish to achieve greater intimacy as a couple, but find it difficult to communicate with each other. Talk about how you might do this. For example, you may decide that you both want to have more conversations about each partner's day so that you each have a better understanding of what the other does, what they are going through and how they feel about. Talk about how you can achieve this. Perhaps you might decide that short conversations over dinner everyday may be a good start. You may also decide that you would like to set aside some time during the week or schedule time for a walk together so that you can talk more at length. As you talk about this, you might see that other activities or that other family members' needs might have to be considered in order for you to be able to set aside some time to spend together. These talks will help you define what it is you want to achieve and how you will be able to do it, which, in turn, will help you come up with a specific action plan.

While working with an action plan is the best way to attain your goals, it is important to consider that sometimes, it may not always go as smoothly as you would wish. You may find that you need to adjust your action plan once you start talking about how it may affect your lives. Learning to design an action plan that takes into consideration your needs, as an individual, as well as, those as a couple will help you to establish a good foundation for achieving future goals. This is a part of being more effective and thoughtful within your relationship.

When you put together an action plan, think about the advantages, as well as, any disadvantages in it. For example, you decide to live within a budget, in order to save money for a house. The advantages may include knowing exactly how much money you will save and feeling good about being able to make plans for the near future. The disadvantages may involve not taking a costly holiday or changing your casual spending habits. It is important to weigh up the various issues that may arise as a result of working toward your aims, so that you can be prepared for them.

If you or your partner fall short of achieving a goal, don't put yourselves down or start blaming each other. Your life together is not about what a failure you are or who can be more perfect than the other. Instead, discuss calmly what has occurred. You may need to redefine the goal, break it down into smaller goals or reset the time scale for it. Ask each other, *"How can I help you achieve the goal?"* Listen to the reply and try to act on it. This is what we mean by being thoughtful, helpful and reasonable to be effective so that you can achieve your goal, and feel happy for doing so.

Sometimes, it may be difficult to follow your specific action plan due to unavoidable or unforeseen circumstances. If this happens, review the situation as soon as possible. You may need to revise your action plan for a short period of time or change its entire time scale.

When you or your partner achieve a particular goal, make a point of noting it – and allow yourself to celebrate it! Telling each other how much you appreciate even the smallest efforts indicates that you value each other and helps to build confidence within your relationship.

Deciding on priorities

Each new day brings with it a series of duties, tasks and activities in which we take part. Try as we might, it is not possible to be in two places at the same time or even do two things at once, at least not with any great effectiveness. We tend to prioritize activities as we go along, deciding on the things that need to be done first and on the ones that can wait. It is important to decide what your priorities are so that you can plan and live, accordingly. Learning to make effective plans that include appropriate and mutual priorities will help you to structure your life in a helpful way. This can bring about positive changes in your relationship, as you both invest your energy and work together on mutually identified priorities.

We all have different priorities, but if your aim as a couple is to build a better relationship, doing the exercises and spending time together will help you come closer as a couple.

Prioritize your aims and goals. These can be individual aims and goals, as well as, those that you have set yourselves to achieve together.

Consider both your practical and emotional needs when deciding on your priorities. It is helpful if you can work towards achieving a healthy sense of balance in your life.

Time and money management

In the last part of this chapter, we talk about time and money management. While there are many issues that can have an effect on couples and their relationship, time and money are probably the two that can affect a couple in almost every way, from the practical to the emotional aspects of their life together. When not handled effectively, time and money can become the source of stress and trouble within a relationship. In this section, we discuss the need for effective management of time and money as part of a strong partnership.

Please note – there are many excellent sources of books or the internet that will guide you through how to manage your time or set up an appropriate budget and how to invest for your financial future. You may find it helpful to use them.

Time management

One of the most common symptoms of modern life is lack of time. Most people lead hectic lives, rushing from one activity to the next. As you yourself are probably all too aware, it is very easy to let our lives run us, instead of us feeling in control of our lives. Lack of time is often a key source of stress in a couple's relationship. Managing time effectively not only helps us use it more efficiently, but it is also an essential part of a successful partnership.

It is often easy to underestimate the amount of time and effort we need in order to start and keep a process of change going. We tend to expect that we can easily manage our time to accommodate our own and our partner's needs and probably, the needs of multiple others in our life. It may help both, you and your partner, to become aware that there is a real need to make a commitment with regards to allocating time for each other. Having done so, you may find that it is no easy task at first, to juggle your respective work commitments alongside the various activities, family and social commitments that make up your lives, in order to create time to be together.

Use the worksheets to help you work through your time management issues. Doing the worksheets can highlight specific problem areas, which in turn, can help you as a couple to reorganize your time or alter your unrealistic expectations of each other. Keep in mind that creating the time for each other will help your relationship to thrive.

Lisa and Tim

Lisa and Tim are a married couple in their thirties. They both work hard at their jobs. However, Tim's work demands a great deal of his time, with many commitments that extend into the evenings and weekends. Because of this, they were unable to celebrate their anniversary and Lisa feels very negative about their situation.

Lisa identified the event (*see Worksheet One p.90*) that was the cause of her prickly thoughts and negative emotions: Tim's work commitments prevented them from celebrating their anniversary. Her action plan was to sit down and have a talk with Tim about

WORKSHEET ONE
UNDERSTANDING WHAT HAPPENED

NAME	Lisa
EVENT	We didn't celebrate our wedding anniversary, because Tim had work commitments that evening.
PRICKLY THOUGHTS	He does not have enough time for us. I find myself wondering if he cares whether we spend time together.
EMOTIONS & FEELINGS	Frustration Anger
RATING	9/10 9/10
WHAT I WANT TO CHANGE	I need to talk to Tim about how I feel.

how she felt. They decided to talk about it the next day, as both of them understood what was happening.

They had a discussion about it the next day (*see Worksheet Two, p.92–3*). This was good timing. They did not try to have the discussion late at night when Tim returned from his business meeting and when Lisa's emotions were running high, but getting more manageable after Tim said sorry. They waited until the next day when they both had a chance to sit down earlier in the evening to talk about it. Also, because the discussion took place the next day, they did not leave too much time between the event and their discussion, which is also helpful in resolving problems. They further made sure that their meeting was not disrupted and that it took place in comfortable surroundings.

In the section *Discuss Together* they listed what they felt they needed to talk about. They both approached this with an open mind and they did not make assumptions about what should have happened. They also identified some changes they needed to make. In the *What we are going to do* section they came up with suggestions about what they might be able to do in the future to avoid a repetition of the previous night's event. They decided on much more communication about their schedules so that they could plan better. They also decided to review the situation in one month's time to see how well these changes were working for them.

After one month (*see Worksheet Three, p.95–6*), Lisa and Tim talked about how they felt about their schedules and the time they had for each other. Overall, they were communicating much better and felt quite positive about the changes they had made. They also came to understand the need for flexibility and the fact that, sometimes, they just had to accept that certain situations

WORKSHEET TWO
WHAT WE ARE GOING TO DO

EVENT	*We didn't celebrate our wedding*	
NAME	*Lisa*	*Tim*
	I want Tim to understand that I felt really upset that he couldn't make the time to go out and celebrate.	*I had an important business meeting to attend. I want Lisa to understand that my work is important to me and to us as a family, but I also want to help her feel that I'm there for her.*
WHAT WE WANT TO CHANGE	*We want to change the current situation where Lisa doesn't feel she can make any plans, because they can always be cancelled at the last minute.*	

WORKSHEET TWO
(CONT.)

WHAT WE ARE GOING TO DO	We will try and combine our social and business diaries We will plan ahead so that Tim can take time off if necessary or at least not schedule meetings on evenings when we have something planned. We will try to communicate our needs as far in advance as possible.
SET A DATE TO DO WORKSHEET THREE – WHERE WE ARE NOW	6th December

were not changeable or ideal. By working through the worksheets, identifying the changes they needed to make and following through on their action plan, they were able to feel more positive and relaxed with each other. Also, allocating more time to each other enabled each partner to feel valued by the other and they felt more satisfied in their relationship

Money management

As with time, money plays a large part in most of our lives and it can take on an added significance when it involves another person. It is well known that money is a topic that commonly causes arguments and stress within a relationship. If money is an area, which becomes associated with problems in a partnership, it is usually not the money itself that is the root of the distress, but how it is managed. Working through the worksheets can help you to identify the underlying causes of your thoughts, behaviours and feelings with regards to money. At the same time, doing the money management worksheets can help you to begin to manage money more effectively, so that it eventually becomes a positive aspect of your relationship, rather than a hindrance.

If money is an issue for you or your partner, think about the place money takes in your lives. What do you want from your money? How do you want to use it? What are your thoughts and emotions about money? Consider these questions to open up discussions that will help you to identify the causes of your problems with money.

Get to know your money. You need to learn how much income you have and what your outgoing expenses are. Talk about this

WORKSHEET THREE
WHERE WE ARE NOW

NAME	*Lisa and Tim*
DATE	*6th December*
WHAT ARE MY THOUGHTS NOW?	*We've spent more time discussing and negotiating our schedules.* *We have clearer communication.* *We've achieved more flexibility between ourselves and a better understanding of the issues.*
HOW DO I FEEL NOW?	*We feel that we can communicate better.* *We feel we are able to spend more quality time together.* *We are not arguing as much as before.*
EMOTIONS & FEELINGS	*We feel a lot happier than before.*
RATING	*7/10*

WORKSHEET THREE
(CONT.)

HOW MUCH THE EVENT HAS BEEN RESOLVED?

We've been able to discuss the actual dispute and put it to rest. However, we realise that we need to continually balance the time we spend with each other with our work demands.

IS THERE ANY FURTHER ACTION REQUIRED?

Our commitments to maintaining progress are:

(1) To communicate our needs to each other in a timely fashion
(2) Accept that certain situations are not changeable or ideal
(3) Come up with alternatives whenever possible
(4) Follow through the plans we make
(5) Re-commit to each other if that is what is required.

with each other so that you both have a clear understanding of your money. It is important for you to both know how much money you have, how much money you owe, how much you need to spend on necessities, how much you need to save and how much you may have left to spend on something you enjoy.

If managing money is an issue, you need to commit to becoming more aware of how you spend your money. Compare different ways in which you can use your money so you become more efficient at managing it. For example, perhaps you simply take money out of the bank throughout the week when you need cash without being aware of how much you are spending. Or perhaps you do not keep receipts so you do not have a clear idea of how you spend your cash. It might be helpful for you to pay for everything using your debit or credit card for a week so that you have a record on your statement of how much cash you spent and how you spent it. Alternatively, you could keep a diary of all your expenditures or you might even buy a money management programme, which you could use on your computer.

Remember that using money can be emotional, as well as, just practical. For example, you might go on a shopping spree when you are feeling depressed or, conversely, because you are feeling happy about something. You may find yourself spending money on your partner or children when you feel guilty about not having enough time for them or because you expressed anger over something that happened. Some people behave irresponsibly with money, because they are afraid to take responsibility for their financial security.

Do try to become more aware of the reasons behind how you use your money. Practise using money in a positive and responsible way:

> *If managing money is problematic for you, you could draw up a budget for short-term and long-term expenditures. A budget will allow you to prioritize what you want to do with your money and work towards your goal.*

> *If you are on a tight budget and lack the money for spontaneous expenditures, you may feel depressed or resentful. While it is valid to feel this way, try to change your perspective, rather than focusing on these negative emotions. For example, you might feel sad or inadequate, because you cannot buy or expect to receive a bouquet of exotic flowers. If that is the case, think about the love and consideration that goes into gathering a bunch of flowers from your garden or wildflowers from a field.*

> *While it is worthwhile to be able to save money for a big expenditure, remember to allow a little room in your budget for occasional small expenditures.*

> *However much money you may have and whatever way you decide to manage your money, consider setting aside a certain amount for each person to spend in whatever joyful way they like. This method can be especially useful for couples trying to live within a budget.*

> *Reward yourselves for successfully following the action plan that you have designed together. Celebrate the fact that you have managed your money well.*

How to get the most out of your conversations with each other

The previous chapters have shown you how you can use the CBT approach to help you to identify the problem areas in your relationship and resolve the issues you may be experiencing.

In this chapter, we introduce different strategies and activities that can enhance the whole process. We will talk about the best ways to remain focused during your conversations and how to communicate effectively. We will also explore the positive changes you can make in your daily lives so that you can cope better. This, in the long run, can have a significant positive impact on your relationship.

Follow a format

The first thing you need to do together is to decide when and where you will have your conversation about the issues. Choose a time and place that is comfortable and private and where you will not be interrupted. It is not advisable to have difficult talks very late at night or over a meal or when children or others are present. Those times are leisure times when you might allow yourself to enjoy them as such. If you decide to have your talk with each other at home, ensure that your children are being looked after. If your children are being looked after in your house while you are talking, it is important that the children feel positive rather than concerned about your time together. It might be best to meet when you know they are with friends enjoying themselves, for example. Ensure that you turn off your phones, the television and radio, that you put away any work or other distractions and give each other your undivided attention. Some couples prefer a more neutral place, like a coffee shop or the park. The most important thing is for it to be a place where you can feel relaxed and at ease with each other.

Consider how long your conversation might be. It is better if you keep it limited to about an hour or so to avoid getting too tired, which can affect you both emotionally and mentally.

Next, decide together what you would like to talk about with each other. It is important that you agree on specific issues that are important to you as a couple. If you have not yet done so, please read through Chapter Three – Assessing the Situation and do the exercises we suggest so that you have a clear idea of what you feel the problems are that need to be worked on.

Once you agree on the topic that you both wish to discuss, write it down and refer to it. If you find that you would like to do some work on the worksheets before talking to each other, let the other know and do this. Keep your conversations focused on what you have agreed to explore. If, at any time, other problems come up which you feel need attention, jot them down and add them to the topics you want to discuss. You could then allocate some time to the new topic in the future.

When deciding on what you will focus on each time, it is helpful to try to keep it specific or break it down so that you can have a good conversation about it during that time. If the topic is too general or too big, it can be difficult to resolve anything or to feel that you are progressing. Try to come to some sort of a conclusion by the end of each session even if it is not necessarily one that always results in the issues being resolved. A successful conversation is one that helps you to understand better what you both think and feel about an issue. When the conversation generates ideas about changes you might make or ways of doing things differently in relation to the topic that you have been exploring, it is a good conclusion, because you have reached a point where you are working together. Allow yourselves to feel good about this. Doing so will also help you to act on these changes and enable you to try out things in a different way. The next time you get together to follow up on your original conversation, remember to talk with each other about how these changes or different ways of doing things have worked for each one of you.

It would be helpful if you could try to schedule at least one regular conversation every week, while you are working through specific problems. Once or even twice a week conversations are useful in giving each other the necessary feedback and support. Write this time down in your diaries and make it a priority to honor this as a commitment to each other and your relationship. Arrange your schedule in a way that this time remains reserved for each other.

At the end of each meeting, acknowledge what you feel you have achieved. Please remember that these focused talking times are part of an on-going process. There may be times when you feel more positive about it than at other times. This is to be expected and is perfectly okay. The very fact that you are working together as a couple is a great accomplishment and you will notice progress over time. Whenever possible, make plans to do something relaxing together after these talks. Sometimes, having something pleasurable to look forward to, can help you to get through the exploration of difficult topics.

Be focused

Once you agree on the topic you want to explore, stay focused on it. The time you set aside is essentially your time to sort out the problem. You have a far better chance of resolving a problem if you focus on it and explore it in detail. It may also be easier to stick to the point if you know your exploration is time-limited. As we have suggested previously, please do not allow this process to go on for hours. Plan for about an hour.

If you realize that you and/or your partner have drifted away from the topic you chose to focus on, point it out in a kind manner, without making judgments about yourself or your partner. Say something like, "We seem to have gotten away from the topic. Let's make a note of what we ended up talking about so that we can talk about it at a later time if we feel we need to." Be mindful that you do not start accusing each other of being self-centered or putting yourself down about not being able to focus. All these judgments will take you away from the topic at hand and get in the way of accomplishing positive outcomes.

If you find yourselves drifting away repeatedly from your topic of exploration, take a few moments and try to understand why this is happening. You may discover that you are using this tactic to avoid talking about the real problem. Perhaps the actual problem is difficult or painful to talk about. If so, acknowledge that this is the case, but do try to talk about it step by step. Be aware of your coping point (which we explain to you later in this chapter) so that it does not become too distressing. Tell each other when you feel you need a break. Acknowledge and accept what the other person is saying and then come back to your exploration.

Sometimes, the topic you have chosen to discuss touches emotions or brings out issues that are bigger and more painful than you might initially have anticipated. If this happens, you need to talk about this situation with each other. If you both decide that you feel you can work through these emotions and issues together, then try to work through them. You might find that not only is it useful to talk about these emotions, but that having them as an integral part of your conversations helps you to understand each other better. In Chapter Five – How to use the worksheets we talk about John and Tara who undergo a similar situation.

Sometimes, however, the issues are just too painful, especially when they touch on traumatic incidents or trigger severely distressing childhood experiences. If this is the case, then we strongly advise you to seek professional help.

Ground rules for couples

As you start to examine the relationship difficulties that you may be experiencing, it is helpful to establish some simple ground rules for yourself and in your interactions with each other.

Commit to change. Each partner must want to change and be willing to make a sincere commitment to the process.

Respect yourself and each other. This includes allowing your partner the time to speak without interrupting and to accept that what your partner has shared is your partner's truth and belief. Don't judge it even if you don't agree with it. You are entitled to have a different view and respect implies that you can share this, too.

Recognize the need to deal with difficult issues. Both partners must also really want to resolve them in a way that is mutually accepting of the other.

Decide on your goals. Be prepared to negotiate and allow space for each other when deciding on goals.

Learn and use good communication skills. (This is explained in the next section.)

Avoid blaming yourself and each other. Help each other to stay focused on the issue instead and be supportive of each other.

Be non-judgmental about yourself and towards each other. Be aware of any judging thoughts or negative assumptions, which you may hold and recognize these to be unhelpful to yourself and your partner. Instead, allow yourself to focus on the issue. Being non-judgmental will also help make you feel more secure with each other and you will be able to express yourselves more freely.

Be courteous with each other. Be tactful in the way you express yourself and consider each other's feelings.

Decide in whom you will confide and how much you will tell others about certain aspects of your relationship. Make this into a mutual confidentiality agreement.

Try not to revisit or to revive past issues. Doing so will distract you and get in the way from helping you to resolve the issue at hand.

Do not react to your emotions by taking them out on your partner. Sometimes, you may find that what your partner does or says triggers strong emotions in you, for example, anger or some other intense emotional pain. If you do feel this way, recognize that these are your own emotions, acknowledge them, but do not act on them in relation to your partner.

Make your exploration and discussions time-limited, especially when you are working on a difficult issue.

If you wish, you can add to the above ground rules or make your own set of ground rules to use in your interactions with each other. Decide together what they should be and then write them down.

You may also like to write out an agreement, so that you can remind yourselves of your commitment to change and to follow the ground rules. And above all, enjoy the progress that you make!

Effective communication in a relationship

Using good communication skills will help your conversations to be effective and calm. It will also be instrumental in bringing the two of you closer together. Good communication between partners is essential in building a strong relationship and it is especially necessary when conflicts arise. Without good communication skills, the existing problems are made worse, because they are not expressed in a manner, which can be understood by the other. Good communication is more than just talking. It involves being responsive. Listening, accepting, discussing and negotiating are the keys to understanding each other.

To help you achieve this, commit to and aim to follow these guidelines in all your interactions:

Have good eye contact with your partner.

Use 'I' instead of 'you' statements. For example, *"I feel angry when you are late!"* instead of *"You make me feel angry when you are late!"*

Use precise language when speaking. Avoid jargon in order to convey a clear message. It is not clear simply to say that you want things to be different or that you want a happy and/or peaceful life: you need to explain specifically what this means to you. Keep focused on the topic.

Listen to each other and avoid interrupting. Take this in turns, in order to give each other the opportunity to speak and be listened to.

Accept what the other person says even if you disagree. Then, talk about why you disagree with what has been said. Aim to negotiate a positive conclusion. In the next section, we discuss acceptance in greater detail.

You can really support your partner and show them that you understand what they have said by summarizing it back to them.

Avoid making assumptions. Ask questions to learn what the other person is thinking and feeling. Ask questions to clarify anything you don't understand.

Refrain from arguing or becoming defensive. If strong feelings get triggered, just recognize them, but don't respond.

Be aware of your own and your partner's thoughts, emotions, actions and body movements. Ask for clarification if you don't understand these in a particular situation.

Focus on what you and your partner need or want. Steer away from what you think you or your partner should do. 'Shoulds' are often veiled assumptions about yourself or your relationship and are unhelpful.

Be non-judgmental of yourself and each other. Judgement is always based on assumptions, which frequently do not match reality. Allow yourself to be accepting of and open with each other.

Acceptance

We outlined above that an important part of good communication is accepting what your partner is saying. Acceptance does not necessarily mean that you agree with what has been said. It means that you understand what is being said. For example, imagine that your partner says to you, "I'm upset because you were late coming home." You might feel this statement is unfair. Perhaps you came home at what you felt was a reasonable time or it may be you had discussed earlier that day that you would be coming home later than usual and your partner forgot. When two people have different perceptions of an event, it is all too easy to start arguing about it.

The essential thing to do in this circumstance is to validate what your partner is saying and feeling. Saying something like, *"I'm sorry you're feeling upset, let's talk about it!"* shows that you accept and empathize with what your partner is feeling. Likewise, for the partner who has just had their statement or feelings validated, it is important to acknowledge it. For example, *"I really appreciate you telling me that you want to talk about it!"* indicates to the other person that you recognize their efforts to understand. Then, you can go on to have a discussion to clear up any misunderstanding that may have occurred.

Establishing your coping point

At various times in our lives, we have to deal with stressful situations. It is important to know what we can cope with. This is our coping point.

It is essential to recognize what you can cope with. For example, you may wake up with a slight headache one morning, but you know you will still be able to go to work and do your job properly. You are within your coping limits. However, on another day, you may wake up with a high temperature and feel very unwell in which case you know you will not be able get up and function appropriately. In this situation, you have reached your physical coping point and need to take responsibility for taking time to get well. Once you have recovered sufficiently, you will have the strength to return to your normal daily routine. If, on the other hand, you choose to go beyond your coping point, you may find yourself becoming very seriously ill.

In the same way, we need to be mindful of our emotional state of well being. As an example, imagine that you and your partner are having a conversation about a painful problem in your relationship. You may start to feel negative emotions but feel you are able to cope with them. As the conversation continues, you feel your anxiety levels rise to what you know is your coping point. You need to communicate this to your partner so that you can take a break from the discussion at this time. Again, as with the physical coping point, if you choose to ignore your emotional coping point, you risk becoming so distressed that you will not be able to function effectively in the conversation.

If we ignore our coping point and go beyond the level of stress we can cope with, we approach the point when we feel that we simply cannot take anymore. This is the cut-off point. Ignoring your coping point and moving towards the cut-off point can lead you to respond in ways, which you may later regret, such as becoming verbally or physically abusive.

The coping point and cut off points are different for everyone. For example, people who are in robust good health with a positive outlook may be able to endure a great deal of physical and mental hardship compared to others who are frail and have a long history of poor health. We also have different coping point and cut off points for stress, anxiety and distressing emotions. Some people seem to have a natural ability to cope with a great deal of stress, while others cannot handle it to the same degree.

As you can see from the graph (*see p.110*) the emotional coping point is approximately halfway between feeling no anxiety at zero (0) and feeling completely distressed at ten (10). Learning to recognize how you feel as you approach your coping point is a very useful skill that will help you to manage your distressing feelings.

The time it takes to reach the coping point and cut-off point can vary, depending on our state of health, the level of tiredness or how much stress we have already experienced that day. This is one of the reasons why we suggest that you try to have your conversations at a time of day when neither of you are too tired. How quickly we reach the coping point can even vary according to the topic being discussed.

Once the coping point is reached, it is necessary to take a break from the discussion so that the anxiety levels can come down. In this book we have discussed some basic strategies on how to calm yourselves when anxiety levels go up.

If you are mindful of your own and your partner's coping point and treat yourselves and each other with respect, the time for recovery is much faster than if you ignored it. Once the anxiety level falls you will feel less emotional and you can resume your conversation. Getting to know your own coping point and

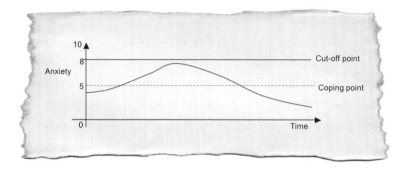

becoming sensitive to your partner's coping point is an important step towards resolving issues. Despite your increased ability to read each other's coping point, it will still be important that you always tell each other when you are approaching your own emotional coping point. Never assume that the other person should be able to know how you are feeling! It is always your responsibility to let them know. Showing respect for yourselves and each other will also help boost your self-esteem and confidence in each other. It will enable you to feel comfortable and safe in each other's presence.

Using negotiation skills in a relationship

Negotiation is something we do everyday and, generally speaking, the more skilled we are at it, the easier time we have in our interactions with people. To negotiate appropriately is a very important part of any relationship. Negotiating means talking about what each of you feel you need and want and being flexible so that you can accommodate each other's needs.

We all have needs and wants and we try to get them met. Clashes can occur when each of us wants something different. Here is a common example. Let's say you and your partner go to the cinema one evening. Sometimes you both want to see the same film, so there is no need to negotiate whose choice it will be. However, what happens if you want to see different films? Well, you can choose to be inflexible and argue about it and risk turning the evening into an unpleasant experience where you both end up feeling resentful, or, you can negotiate. Perhaps you decide to see one of the two choices this week and the other the next week. Alternatively, you could both decide to see a completely different film, something that is closer to both your tastes. You may even decide that you would both be perfectly happy seeing your choices separately, sometimes. However, be careful not to make this into a regular habit, as it is important for your relationship to spend leisure time together.

Once you make your decision together, be gracious about it. In other words, it really is not helpful to the relationship for one partner to talk negatively about how they compromised on what they wanted. Such behaviour only leads to resentment. Using the above example, if you decide to see a film that is not your first choice, allow yourself to enjoy it. Even if, after seeing the film, you did not enjoy it, don't criticize your partner for their selection or say that you would have been better off seeing your choice. Remind yourself that the next film will be one that you choose and that you wouldn't like it if your partner made negative comments about your preferred choice. If each negotiation led to this sort of criticism, your partner could end up feeling inhibited in expressing their needs and wants.

Good negotiation involves all the skills we discussed in the section on good communication. It is important to listen carefully to each other, validate each other's feelings and be an effective communicator. If you use positive words and open-ended questions, your partner will feel that you are open to suggestion.

Open-ended questions are those that give each partner the opportunity to express themselves. These kinds of questions allow you to reply beyond a simple *"yes"* or *"no"*. Instead, they encourage you to elaborate on your thoughts, present more information and even be more creative in your perspective. For example, if you ask your partner: *"Do you want to eat pasta tonight?"* your partner will say either *"yes"* or *"no"* in answer to your question. However, if you ask, *"What would you like to eat tonight?"* your partner can answer in all sorts of ways. This question can open up a discussion about what sort of meal you both would like or perhaps whether it might even be a good idea to go out to eat. Another example of a question, which does not always allow one much room for discussion is, *"Did you have a good day today?"* Again this type of question can only be answered with *"yes"* or *"no"*. If, on the other hand, you ask, *"What was your day like today?"* your partner can give you more information about the day and how they feel about it. So, when you ask open-ended questions it not only helps you to gather information, it gives you the opportunity to discuss matters and, if necessary, carry on to problem-solving conversations.

Words are very powerful. They can be positive and soothing, creating happy and calming effects or they can cause negative and prickly sensations, resulting in feelings of unhappiness, insecurity and anger. Words can even make or break a relationship. Using positive words in your conversation will help you and your partner to inspire and motivate each other. Doing so will help both of you to build confidence in yourselves and in your relationship. When negative words or statements are used, it is not uncommon to feel hurt and sad. This is counterproductive, because it will not inspire you or your partner to do something positive about a troubling situation. Generally speaking, negative words and statements are unhelpful and can be detrimental to the relationship.

Consider the following example. Your partner has cooked something new and it has not turned out the way you like it. If your comment is, *"This is no good, it is overcooked!"* you will most likely hurt your partner's feelings. It might even discourage them from trying to develop their skills. If, instead, you say, *"It looks okay, I look forward to tasting it. I think it's great that you tried to make this difficult dish!"* you are acknowledging your partner's efforts and encouraging them to continue to expand their proficiency.

Another common example of a negative statement is when one person says to the other, *"You hardly ever listen to me!"* This sort of comment can lead to a senseless exchange, such as, *"Yes, I do!"* and, *"No, you don't!"* At the very least, this is hardly conducive to inspiring each other to listen better. A more positive comment would be, *"You do listen to me sometimes!"* This positive assertion will alert your partner that they may not always feel listened to and help both of you to explore how much you do listen to each other. This will enable you to become more attentive toward each other, because you feel good in each other's company.

Sometimes, we need time to think about how we feel or what we want. Therefore, it is important that you learn to be patient with each other and not to push your partner into making choices when they are not ready to do so.

Make sure you are negotiating on realistic and achievable goals. For example, if you are planning a holiday together, keep in mind each person's preferences regarding the environment and climate, as well as, how much you can afford financially and in terms of time away from work or home. Be prepared to explain your choices and listen to what is being discussed.

Good negotiation means understanding both sides of the discussion and coming up with the best alternatives that will help you to move forward together.

Ultimately, good negotiation will help you to understand yourself and your partner better. This, in turn, will help you to work more collaboratively with each other. As you become more skilled in negotiation, you will find you are able to achieve more successful conclusions and feel more satisfied in your relationship.

Susan and James

The following illustration involving Susan and James shows the importance of effective communication. Through developing their communication and negotiating skills, this couple was able to explore their thoughts, feelings and emotions and the impact these had on their relationship. They used the worksheets to facilitate the process.

Susan and James are a couple who experienced negative emotions due to a lack of communication about a domestic issue in their lives. Susan was feeling low and felt generally that James was uncaring about her. James was surprised to learn that Susan felt this way, since she had never expressed any dissatisfaction with his behaviour towards her. He said he felt he demonstrated a lot of consideration for Susan, doing his share of the household chores and going so far as to get frequent take-away meals for them to share together to save them the time and effort to prepare their evening meals. When asked to consider what it was about James' behaviour that she found uncaring, Susan replied that she expected him to take her out for the occasional meal at their local hotel. She wanted him to plan the time to be together and for them to dress up and make a special occasion out of the evening. These are what she considered demonstrations of care and affection. She felt let down when James persisted in bringing home take-away meals, instead of arranging a special evening just for the two of them.

After exploring this event, they uncovered the underlying reason for the negative emotions in the relationship. Both lacked the ability to communicate their needs to each other. Not only had Susan not communicated her expectations to James, she had also not expressed how she felt when these expectations were not realized. By working through the worksheets, they were able to understand the importance of effective communication.

Both James and Susan were able to accept the importance Susan placed upon occasionally getting away from the usual scene of their home. She wanted to be in an elegant, formal setting that required special effort for them to be able to attend and afford this. Through improving their communication, Susan and James learned to identify the areas in their lives that could be planned and organized better, so that they did not have to rely on buying expensive take-away meals at the end of long day at work. They were then able to save up for the occasional expensive meal in a special setting. By learning to reorganize the practical aspects of their life, they were able to fulfill each other's emotional needs and create a positive outcome.

Although Susan and James realized that they needed to make changes in their lifestyle to be able to fulfill Susan's needs, they were initially resistant towards making these changes. James felt it would take too long before they could afford the evening out. Susan felt it was too difficult to try to plan their meals for the entire week. Neither enjoyed shopping for groceries or cooking after a hard day at work. Again, working with their worksheets on their thoughts and emotions on this matter, they were able to see that their fears and anxieties about the proposed changes were holding them back from making them. James feared that they would never have enough money and Susan felt anxious about failing to become better organized.

If fear and anxiety are present in your relationship, these will be the most likely factors for any resistance to change. Identifying and acknowledging them is the first step to overcoming any resistance.

Once Susan and James identified what they were feeling anxious about, they decided to find out what strategies and action plan would be useful in helping them to overcome these feelings. By using their time and money management worksheets, they were able to break down their goals and tasks so that they were able to manage them more easily. They learned to cope on a practical level by doing things differently, as explained, below, and, consequently, they were able to deal with their fears and anxieties.

As with any change, changes in your domestic life as a couple may be better met if there is agreement about the need for and the benefits of change. You may also find it easier to undertake and respond positively to the changes if there are tangible incentives.

Susan and James had a reason for change and understood some of the emotional barriers towards that change. Once they were committed to the need for change, it became easier for them to make those changes, especially as they could see some immediate benefits. Not only were they saving money for their long-range goal, they were able to restructure their week so that they could shop when they were not so exhausted. Susan became more adept at planning ahead and they both shared in the cooking at home, which brought an added pleasure to their lives. They also found that by cooking some meals ahead of time and storing spares in the freezer for other days, they actually had more time to spend with each other on other activities.

Negotiation is essential when one partner feels they will 'lose out', as a result of the change. In their effort to help themselves budget more efficiently, Susan and James decided to discontinue using their credit cards. While James felt that living on a small cash allowance every week presented no hardship, Susan felt that not having credit facilities was an extra hardship for her. She pointed out that James's lifestyle would hardly change at all since he tended to use cash anyway and was not responsible for doing the bulk of the weekly shopping in the same way as she was. Susan felt it would be an additional burden on her time and energy if she had to go in search of a cash machine with their young children every time she needed to make a purchase. Susan also explained that one of the advantages to using a card over cash was that they had a record of how they had spent their money, which they found useful. After some negotiation, Susan and James decided to set up a debit account with a debit card that Susan could use to pay for monthly essentials. This helped them to feel in greater control over their finances and, yet, met Susan's needs for ease of access.

Whatever the situation, if there is a need for change, the outcome must offer some benefit to both parties. Therefore for any situation you want to change, allow yourself to explore the potential benefits with an open mind.

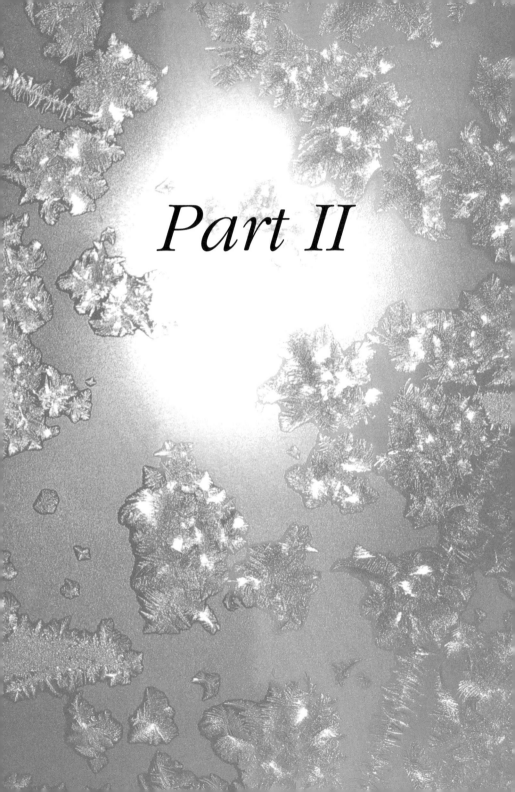

Part II

Activities to enhance your well-being

In the following section, we explore activities that can help enhance your well-being. You may wonder why we are including this information in a book about resolving relationship difficulties. This is because the better you feel about yourself mentally, physically and emotionally, the better you will be able to cope with the demands in your everyday life, including your relationship.

Our focus here is on three areas. The first is to help you to develop your ability to relax and feel more calm; the second looks at your general health; the third includes a selection of activities you could do together to help you rediscover and strengthen the positive bonds you share in your relationship.

Relaxation, focusing the mind and being mindful

Being relaxed, focusing the mind and being mindful are important states of being. They help you to become aware of yourself - your thoughts, emotions and behaviors and how you perceive what is happening around you. Being aware is essential to creating a non-judgmental relationship with yourself and others. Looking at yourself in a non-judgmental way will help you to accept your present reality more lovingly.

Relaxation

Relaxation is a skill that can be learned. The key to relaxation is breathing. In our fast paced lives we tend to shallow breathe, taking in less oxygen than is beneficial for us. Continuous shallow breathing can make us feel tired and tense. Deep breathing helps your lungs, because it helps you take in lots of fresh air and oxygen, which in turn, refreshes your body and relaxes your mind.

Here is a simple method to practice basic relaxation:

> *Choose a quiet place. Lie down on the floor or sit in a comfortable chair. Make sure that you sit up, so that you are not slouching. Loosen any tight clothing like belts or ties.*

> *Allow your stomach to move out when you inhale and move in as you exhale, like air going in and out of a balloon. Do not hold your breath; just inhale and exhale. Allow yourself to breathe slowly. There is no need to rush.*

> *Focus on the breath coming in and going out. It may be helpful to count to four as you breathe in and count to four again as you breathe out.*

> *Try to practice this relaxation two or three times a day and spend at least five minutes per session. Aim to do this exercise before eating. Otherwise, wait at least for two hours or longer after a meal.*

> *If you have difficulty falling asleep or simply wish to feel more relaxed as you go to sleep, try practicing this relaxation in bed. Prepare yourself for bed and lie down on your back with your arms along your side and practice this deep breathing.*

While working with the basic relaxation technique, incorporate the following exercises to enhance your relaxation and develop your ability to live mindfully.

Focusing the mind

Focusing your mind will help you to concentrate on your deep breathing. Here are some suggestions:

> *Close your eyes or focus on a specific object in the room. Think of something that you find very pleasant, such as a beautiful sunset or the colour and fragrance of a rose. Focus on the feelings that you connect with the image that you have thought about. Imagery can help you to relax.*

> *If your mind starts to wander, simply acknowledge the thought and bring your mind back to your breathing. It may be helpful to count by 1000s as you breathe in and out. Try counting 1000, 2000, 3000 up to 5000 as you breathe in and up to 6,000 as you breathe out. If you lose track, don't criticize yourself; simply start again.*

> *Another way to focus your mind is to do a focused walk. While walking, take notice of the type of trees around you, the different colours of leaves and flowers. This can help you feel very relaxed.*

> *Explore walking through a field, being especially mindful of your surroundings, the fresh air, the scents, the sounds and the quality of the light around you. This variation is an enjoyable*

exercise to do with your partner. Hold each other's hand as you
both imagine going on this exploratory walk.

Being mindful

Being mindful helps us to react wisely to events. It is about being aware of what we are thinking, doing, saying or experiencing.

Becoming mindful in your interactions with yourself and others will help you to live more fully in the present moment. It is when we are not focused on the present that we begin to think those negative prickly thoughts that lead us into so much difficulty. Being focused on the present moment and what is happening in that moment also helps us to accept ourselves and our partners without being judgmental.

Being mindful also means evaluating your thoughts, as well as, what it is you are experiencing. Instead of making impulsive decisions based solely on your emotions, you will be better able to explore your feelings and your thoughts before rushing into decisions. This will help you to make wiser decisions. Being mindful can also help steer you away from your old ways of getting into arguments, by focusing on your conversation and not judging yourself or each other. By doing so, you and your partner can formulate an appropriate action plan, which can help you to feel better and positive as you address particular issues or problems.

Here are some exercises to learn, which, when practiced regularly, can help you to become more mindful.

First, practice mindfulness daily. Start by focusing on a simple task, which you perform everyday. For example, when you are making a cup of tea try and pay full attention to this process. Notice how your hands lift up the kettle and take it to the tap.

Turn on the tap and listen to the water as it fills the kettle. Be aware of the changing weight of the kettle as it fills with water and so on.

As you simply allow your mind to focus on the present moment, the tension created by the normal rush of thoughts may ease and will allow you to feel relaxed. Another exercise you may find helpful to calm your mind and which you can do at almost any time is to observe yourself massaging your hands. Notice how it feels when you press your hands together, kneading the palm of one hand with the thumb of your opposite hand. Perhaps your fingertips are cold or you discover a spot of stiffness. Become aware of any sensations. You can even be mindful about the raindrops on your window, how these hit the glass, how they splash and then trickle down, taking the other droplets with them. Or you can just watch the snowflakes falling, so light as they fall onto the ground and start to settle, covering the grass or pavement without a sound.

Second, be mindful when you are talking to your partner. Really listen to what they are saying and feeling, really attend and notice your partner being with you talking in the present moment. Be nonjudgmental about the whole event and its process. As you practice this it will become easier with time. Be kind to yourself and do not judge what you are doing by thinking or saying to yourself, *"I am no good at this!"* or, *"I will never be able to do this."* Instead, say to yourself, *"I have tried and next time I will try again and I will do it this way or that way."* You can also be mindful and aware of your partner doing the same, which will allow you to help each other. By being positive and mindful you will start to feel that you and your partner can indeed talk about things without being judged. As you develop to be more mindful, you will most likely discover that you feel more relaxed with each other and better able and willing to cooperate and explore new ideas and alternate ways of resolving problems in your life together. There are an increasing number of books available on mindfulness and you might like to read more about it. We have given you some references to books in Appendix One.

Eating, exercise and sleeping

The three basic activities that affect our physical health are eating (our diet), exercise and sleeping. We not only need an adequate supply of all three to survive, but we need good quality food, exercise and sleep in the right balance to feel well. And why does this matter? Because when we feel well, we experience ourselves more positively and have more energy and can cope better with what we need to do.

Eating

Eating nutritious food helps us to function better physiologically and psychologically. The nutrients found in food boost the chemicals in our brain, which affect not just our physical bodies, but also the way in which we feel. Also, when we eat regular meals, our blood sugar levels are more stable, which also affects how we feel. So, when you eat properly and regularly, you will feel stronger and more positive.

There are so many books and resources available on healthy eating (your doctor, the library, the internet) and therefore, we will not focus on the details here. However, it is neither complicated nor difficult to establish a good routine for yourself. Here are the basics.

Your body feels best if it receives a regular and predictable input of healthy food. Therefore, eating regular meals at regular times is very important. Most people benefit from eating a healthy breakfast, lunch and dinner plus two light snacks, one mid-morning and one mid-afternoon.

Make sure that you are eating a well-balanced diet to get all the nutrients, vitamins and minerals that your body needs. Make healthy choices in what you are eating and drinking. The three main items to look out for are processed sugar, salt and saturated fats. Become aware of how much sugar, salt and saturated fats are in your food and substitute them with healthier options. Look out for the better options of fat, such as unsaturated fats, that do not tend to raise cholesterol levels, and can even lower them, when substituted in place of unhealthy fats. Try cooking food by baking or steaming it, rather than frying in fat or boiling it in water.

In terms of sugars, replace your desire for sweets with eating fruit, instead. For example, eat five portions of fresh fruit and vegetables everyday as recommended by the Department Of Health. Choose fresh fruit, yoghurt or a sandwich for your snacks instead of crisps and sweets. If you have to use sweeteners, use honey instead of processed sugar. Be aware that if you are eating a lot of take-aways or ready-made meals, that there is usually a high level of sugar, salt and unhealthy fat in these foods.

Drink approximately eight glasses of water throughout the day and cut down on stimulants, such as tea, coffee, cola and other drinks containing caffeine. Fruit juice, squash and sodas can also contain a lot of sugar. Be aware of how much alcohol you are drinking. Alcohol, too, contains a lot of sugar and it can act as a depressant. Be aware of your limits and how alcohol affects your mood and your thinking.

Plan ahead so that you have time to shop for food and cook accordingly. Freshly prepared food is so much tastier and nutritious than frozen or ready-prepared meals.

Allow yourself to be mindful and focused on the food, while you eat. You will find mealtimes become a much more pleasant experience. Turn off the television and focus on your meal. Eat slowly and stop eating before you feel too full. This can help prevent you from overeating. One way of being more mindful when eating is to be aware of the texture and taste of the food. Chew your food thoroughly; doing so aids digestion and stops you from overeating.

Keep the conversation light throughout your meal. Meal times are not appropriate for difficult or emotional discussions. Difficult issues need your undivided attention; therefore, it is better if you discuss them at another time. Above all, savour the aromas and tastes and really enjoy your meal and your time together in a pleasant and peaceful atmosphere.

Exercise

Regular exercise has numerous benefits. It not only helps our muscles become and stay fit, it helps our body systems function better. The chemicals our body releases during regular exercise also help to stabilize our moods and make us feel better emotionally.

As with healthy eating, there are many resources available on exercise. It is always a good idea to start by visiting your doctor, before you embark on an exercise programme.

The key to exercise is to keep it simple, within your limits and to engage in an exercise that is enjoyable for you. Start with a goal, which is realistic and achievable. You can build on this as you progress and become more fit. This way, you will feel a sense of achievement from the start and feel good about yourself for exercising. With each new goal you set and achieve, you will gain self-esteem and confidence, along with feeling more energetic.

Write out your plan of exercise, making sure it is practical and realistic for you to follow. For example, if you are new to exercise, you might start with a brisk 15 minutes walk three or four times a week. After two weeks, if you are able to do this easily, you might increase the time to 20 minutes, and so on. Studies show that 30 minutes of brisk walking several times a week is far more beneficial to overall fitness than more frequent intense exercise, so you do not need to feel compelled to take on more than you feel you can handle.

If you find it difficult to feel motivated, add pleasurable features to your exercise, such as going out for a walk with a friend or taking a particularly interesting route. If that is not possible, ask your partner to help you or join a walking club. Sometimes, doing exercise together in a supportive group is very helpful, because in such a setting everyone helps to motivate and inspire each other.

If you can, take regular exercise either in the morning or in the afternoon. According to yoga philosophy, exercise in the morning helps your body to become active and stimulates the brain. If, however, like many people, you exercise in the evening due to time constraints or preference, just be sure to finish your workout with a calming down exercise that will help your mind and body to relax.

Sleep

Sleeping is wonderful. We all know that a good night's sleep helps us to feel refreshed the next day. When we have slept well, we feel calmer and our moods improve so we feel less frustrated. Our concentration levels are better and we pay more attention to what we need to do in our personal and professional lives. As a result, we feel more energetic, motivated, relaxed and happier in ourselves.

Sometimes we may find ourselves waking up in the middle of the night. This is not uncommon. The quality of our sleep changes during the night as we go through the different stages of sleep. The initial stage begins before we fall asleep. This is when our body begins to relax and we start to feel sleepy. The next stage is when we are already asleep and our body and all our muscles start to relax even more. After this, we enter into deep sleep.

Sometimes, we enter into REM (rapid eye movement) sleep. During this phase of sleep we experience our dreams. During REM sleep our body experiences a number of physiological changes, our eyes make movements and brain activity increases. When we have REM sleep, we usually dream. The length of REM sleep changes with age. For example, during infancy and early childhood the percentage of the REM sleep is at its highest and it starts to reduce with age from adolescence to adulthood to midlife and to older age.

The quality of our sleep can change as we move from one sleep phase into another. This is why we sometimes wake up at night. If that happens and you cannot immediately fall back to sleep, do your relaxed breathing. This will help you to go back to sleep within a short while. Also, as we grow older our deep sleep stage shortens and, as a result, we experience lighter sleep during midlife to late life. Again, if you find yourself waking up during the night, do your relaxed breathing.

For some people, having a good night's sleep is more problematic. There are a number of things you can do at home to help you sleep better.

If you do not have a regular pattern of going to sleep, it is important to establish one. Go to bed at a regular time. Set the alarm to wake you up at a regular time each day. This way, even if you have trouble falling asleep, you will wake up at the same time each day. Even if you feel tired during the day due to not having had enough sleep, resist the urge to 'catnap'.

Only allow yourself to sleep when you are actually in your bed. If you are not able to settle and go to sleep within fifteen minutes of having gone to bed, get up and engage in another activity, something relatively calming, such as reading a pleasant book and only go to bed again once you feel sleepy. Once you are in bed do your deep breathing. This will help you to relax even more and make it easier to fall asleep. Repeat this until you can sleep. Eventually, you will start to feel sleepy earlier in the evening so that you will be able to fall asleep when you go to bed.

Sleeping and waking up at regular times is important. Once you have a good regular sleep pattern you will be refreshed the next day.

Drink fewer beverages that contain caffeine throughout the day and try to cut them out altogether especially after five o'clock in the afternoon. Caffeine is a substance that keeps our minds alert and it takes time for it to wear off.

Drink less (if any) alcohol in the evening. Alcohol is a stimulant and keeps your brain active.

If you find you are waking up a few times to go to the bathroom, drink fewer fluids throughout the evening, but make sure you are drinking enough throughout the earlier part of the day. This may help you sleep through the night.

Make your bedroom into a tranquil sanctuary for sleep. Use your bed and bedroom for sleeping. Don't bring your work into it. Take your television out of your bedroom and wherever it is, stop watching it at least half an hour before you get into bed.

Eat healthily and regularly and take regular exercise as we have discussed. This can help you to sleep better, too.

If you are experiencing stress or anxiety, this may prevent you from getting a good night's rest. While it is important to work on these issues, try to do so during the day and use the evening to relax. If you are unable to stop thinking about the things that worry you, try writing down your thoughts and decide that you will deal with them the next morning. Many people find this helpful in managing their worrying thoughts, before they go to sleep. Practice your deep breathing and relaxation regularly before you go to sleep.

There may be other reasons why you are finding it difficult to get yourself to sleep. For example, studies have shown that many people find it difficult to sleep when their bedrooms are too hot. Try turning down or even turn off the central heating and use a lighter blanket. Do not sleep with an electric blanket switched on all night. Open a window for some fresh air. Make sure your room is dark enough. Others find their sleep is disrupted when the weather is too hot or they are too excited, or they have had a very heavy meal late in the evening. Going to bed long after your usual time can also make it difficult to fall asleep.

Various medical conditions can upset your sleep pattern, as can some prescription drugs. Sometimes, sleep can be affected by emotional problems. For example, if you are depressed or suffer from high anxiety due to a very distressing or traumatic experience, it is likely that your sleeping is disturbed. If this is the case, it could be helpful to let your GP know about this and to seek out specialist, professional help to support you with this, if appropriate. You might also find that you are woken by frequent nightmares without having experienced emotional distress or a disturbing event. There are some things you can do about this and we are recommending you talk to your doctor.

Even age affects your sleep as we discussed earlier. Babies have many short sleep cycles throughout the day and night, while teenagers need the most sleep. Adult sleep patterns vary but by retirement age, many people sleep less or wake up earlier.

If you are finding it difficult to sleep, try and find out what the cause of this might be. Some of the positive changes we have suggested may help improve your sleep. If you feel you need additional help, you could contact your doctor for further advice.

Do's and don'ts

We have covered a lot of information in this book about how to identify problem areas and what to do to get through them. Remember, communication is the key to all good relationships. The more you learn to communicate effectively, the more fulfilling your relationship will be. The sign of a good relationship is not a partnership without any problems, but how the people involved choose to deal with issues that arise. A fundamental part of growing together is learning how to communicate and overcome problems.

The following is a list of Do's and Don'ts. If you incorporate them into your day-to-day interactions with each other, they cannot only help you through times of difficulty, but they will serve to enhance your relationship in every way.

> *Ask, rather than assume. Do not expect your partner to be able to read your mind and do not assume you can read theirs.*

> *Refrain from mind reading and making assumptions. Try and be mindful about listening and responding.*

> *Communicate, rather than demand, your needs.*

> *Focus on the positives.*

> *Relax and breathe deeply whenever you can.*

> *Follow the ground rules, as described in Chapter Seven – How to get the most out of your conversations with each other.*

> *Recognize and appreciate each other's efforts, however small they may be. Tell each other how much you appreciate their efforts.*

> *Congratulate yourselves and celebrate your progress! Positive recognition of your achievements is a great motivator.*

> *Take a lead, but do not dominate your partner.*

> *Be focused, but not rigid.*

> *Review and discuss, but do not criticize.*

> *Be gentle with each other.*

> *Be tactful and sensitive to each other's feelings, but do not start avoiding issues.*

> *Be truthful but not judgmental.*

> *Be aware of what is going on for the other, but do not take on the role of their psychotherapist.*

> *Be mindful about what really helps the process.*

> *Magnify the small positive changes, which will help you to progress further.*

> *Move forward. Do not bring up past issues once they have been resolved.*

> *Set a time limit to your work commitments, and work on the priorities in your relationship.*

> *Bring together each other's strengths in order to make your relationship better each day.*

Using different activities

Lack of time is often an overriding issue for one or both partners in a relationship. As a first step towards overcoming this situation, start by setting aside even a few minutes a day to spend together. You may view such a suggestion as counterproductive. After all, you may feel that you already have too many demands on your time and it seems you are being asked to take on another. Yet, your relationship difficulties may stem from the fact that you do not allow yourselves enough time to be with each other.

Relationships are often forged more through frequent and subtle contact rather than elaborate meetings. Think about your own close work relationships or friendships and how these have come about. Did you develop these ties by seeing these people infrequently on a formal basis or through regular proximity? Are you able to talk freely with these people and, if so, how did this ease come about? Most likely it will be because you have spent a good deal of time with these friends and colleagues.

Choose something to do together during the time you have allocated to be together. Prioritize the activities in your daily life. The aim here is to gradually build more time to be together. Once you have planned an activity (whether it is going out for an evening, painting the kitchen or talking about your aims for the long-term future) assess the amount of time and effort you will need for it.

Discuss it, so that you both have a clear idea about how much time the activity will involve. Having a clear and mutual understanding of the time involved in whatever activity you plan for yourselves will help you to enjoy your time together.

Sometimes a change in perspective may be necessary. You and your partner may spend a great deal of time in each other's company, but you may rarely communicate. Even if you spend every minute of the day in each other's company, set aside a few minutes to really talk with each other about how you are feeling.

There are no short-cuts or quick answers when it comes to getting to know another person or ourselves. Avoid trying to speed up this process by trying to do too much all at once. Sometimes the pressures of everyday life, such as the demands of work, family, and friends, can intrude to such a degree that it may seem easier to give up on your time together. It may take some effort coming to terms with each other's needs or differences and this process may not be easy. Remember, however, that opting for the easy way out by avoiding the issues could make the whole process more difficult and time-consuming for you in the long run.

The rationale for spending time together is to help you build towards being happy together as a couple. With practice you will master the necessary skills - communication, patience and tolerance - that will enable you to better understand and appreciate one another.

In this next section we have compiled a variety of activities for you to do together. Each interactive exercise is designed to help you to increase your awareness of each other and to understand the dynamics of your relationship in an enjoyable and creative way. Participating in these activities with each other will help you to share your thoughts, emotions and feelings, which in turn can help you grow together. Growing together opens the way for you to explore and understand the practical and emotional realities of your relationship and will orient you to the present and future needs in your relationship. These exercises are only a starting point. Your imaginations are the only limit!

Here are some guidelines for doing these exercises:

> *Set aside some time when you can both be together, without interruptions or anything competing for your attention.*

> *Take turns answering these questions and really listen to each other's replies.*

> *Be open with each other.*

> *Be non-judgmental with each other.*

Many of the exercises in this section ask you to think and talk about things you may like or want to do. If any of these capture your imagination, act on them.

Try answering a question for your partner and then see how different or similar your answers might be. For example, one question asks you to describe a perfect meal. You know what you would like and you might think you know what your partner would like, but do you really? It might be fun to select a few questions to think about independently of each other, write down the answers and then get together to discuss them.

Do your own homework, rather than asking your partner to do it on your behalf. Think for yourself and be honest with yourself in answering these questions. Don't seek to please your partner with your answers. This is a chance for both of you to be really honest with each other. Being open and allowing your partner to get to know you will help you to work together and enhance your relationship.

Accept what your partner has to say - don't interrupt or finish the sentence for them. Help each other, by being honest and creating a positive and receptive atmosphere. Avoid judging or criticizing each other's replies.

Have fun!

A sample selection of questions and exercises:

> *Ask yourselves – What three experiences would you and your partner like to have in the next year? Write them down and discuss with your partner. You can perhaps make them into your goals or set yourself tasks to work toward achieving them.*

> *What three aspects of your partner's personality do you find attractive?*

> *What three aspects of your own personality do you think your partner finds attractive?*

> *What three aspects of your partner's physique do you find attractive?*

> *Describe the moment when you first noticed your partner or when he/she made an impact on you.*

> *If money were not an object, what gift would you give to*

*your partner? Do you have any emotions associated with this?
If so, talk about them.*

*> Describe an ideal, perfect way of waking up together and try
to weave it into your daily life.*

*> Describe how you would like to spend a sensual morning or
afternoon or evening, with your partner. Where would this take
place? What would this need to entail to make it pleasurable for
you? How can you go about making it happen?*

*> Is there anything you like to do differently before
lovemaking? Are you completely spontaneous or do you like to
set the scene in some way? Discuss your preferences and help
each other fulfill them.*

*> What have you enjoyed recently together that has enhanced
your relationship?*

*> What activities do you enjoy doing together? Do they take
place indoor or outdoors? Whatever they are, choose one to do
together this weekend.*

> Plan to share a hobby, interest or sport with your partner.

*> Write down five of your admirable qualities and five of your
partner's outstanding qualities.*

> Describe three ways you would like to give and take pleasure.

> *Celebrate being together. Celebrate the understanding you have between yourselves.*

> *What three soothing things would you like to be able to do for yourself to help you cope with a difficult situation? If an upsetting situation arises, do these things. Explore with your partner what they would need in such a situation and find out if there are ways in which you could support each other with this.*

> *Try and create a mental catalogue of the good times you have shared together. Consider making a scrapbook of these times and fill it with photographs and mementos or even handwritten thoughts about the experiences.*

> *Try to feel joy and happiness from the little things you share in your life. Bring three such things from the past or the present into your awareness.*

> *Think about your identity as an individual within your relationship as a couple. Explore with each other how each feels about the balance between your time spent as an individual and your time spent as a couple. Does this balance feel about right? If not, what needs changing at this stage? Allow each other to think and talk for themselves when you are doing this.*

> *To feel connected with each other in every way is a tremendous feeling good factor. List three feeling good factors*

in your relationship, which bring you together and help you to feel connected with each other. Think of these things often and celebrate them!

chapter nine

Working through issues

All of us experience a range of emotions everyday. We might wake up in a good mood, but throughout the day, we may undergo stress due to a work situation or feel anxious about our child's progress at school. We may feel rather sad, because a loved one is going through an illness or angry about something we feel is unfair. Then, we might have a positive conversation with a friend or read an uplifting story and we start to feel pretty good about our lives again.

Sometimes, the negative emotions we feel can become magnified and even uncontrollable. That is when they become issues, which can completely affect our outlook and our behaviour. As we illustrated in *Chapter Four – Understanding filters, prickly thoughts and negative emotions*, understanding what issues you may have and working through them will help keep (or put) your relationship on the right track.

The way we think and consequently behave is a key factor in the well-being of all relationships. Prickly thoughts and negative emotions usually affect our behaviour, which, in turn, impacts on the relationship as we illustrated in *Model Two* in *Chapter Two – What is CBT?* As we discussed, sometimes these thoughts and emotions may actually prevent us from understanding our needs. If we, as individuals, cannot identify our own needs, most certainly, it is too much to expect our partner to know what it is we need.

Working through your thoughts and emotions allows you to become more aware of your needs. Being able to identify your needs will help you to feel happier in yourself. This state of mind is a much better platform from which to work on the difficulties you are facing in your relationship. Identifying your needs will also help to motivate you, because you will have some initial goals to work towards.

In this chapter, we will discuss some issues that could be commonly present when couples experience problems in their relationship. These are:

> *Stress and anxiety*
> *Depression*
> *Grief*
> *Anger, frustration and irritability*
> *Jealousy*
> *Your sexual relationship*
> *Mood swings*
> *Medical conditions*
> *Partner dying*

Please remember that these are just a few of the common problem areas people can experience. Also, if at any time you feel that you need the help of a professional therapist, please contact your doctor for an appropriate referral or get in touch with a recognized professional organization, listing their accredited therapists.

Stress and anxiety

Stress and anxiety are feelings we experience in response to something that happens to us. It is quite common to feel some degree of stress everyday. We may feel stress, because we are running late for an important meeting or feel anxious, because we are worried about our partner's health. We may feel sudden stress if we find ourselves in a difficult situation, like driving in very bad weather conditions. In such a situation, stress heightens our awareness so that we can be safe.

There has been a lot written about stress and we may have come to believe that it is always a negative experience. This is not necessarily the case. Stress and anxiety are our normal responses to situations where we feel we need to protect ourselves. Now, it is easy to see how a situation hazardous to us might bring about that sort of response, but what about the stress and anxiety we feel on a daily basis?

The answer to that question is the same. We feel stress and anxiety to protect ourselves. Let us look at a normal event that most of us have experienced at some point in our lives: the anxiety you may feel when you have to take an exam. As the exam day approaches, you may feel stressed. This stress is not trying to protect you from having to take the exam. It is prompting you to respond appropriately to a potentially risky situation. Your anxiety makes you aware that you need to prepare for it. You may then decide to take action and do what you need to do (extra study or training) to be ready for the exam. Even if you have prepared very well, you may still feel some anxiety before the exam, which again, is an instinctive response to help you to be more alert and perform better.

The above can be considered a normal stress reaction. Some people, however, feel so much stress that the feeling overrides everything else in their life to the point that they cannot relax or prepare adequately for the exam. You might have heard people say that their mind goes blank or that they cannot concentrate on what they have to do. This is what we call a negative stress response. This is a totally unhelpful reaction to the situation, because it gives rise to undue anxiety and nervousness.

When anxiety levels go beyond your baseline, it can affect your physical and mental health. Some symptoms of anxiety can be experienced as headaches, breathing difficulties, sweaty palms or even heart palpitations and panic attacks. Anxiety symptoms can cause people to feel very tired. They can also cause changes in a person's thinking process and changes in their mood. People who feel negative stress and anxiety responses are likely to also be experiencing more negative emotions. As a result, if you or your partner are in this situation, there is every chance that you are avoiding certain situations or steering clear of discussing difficult issues in your relationship, which can compound the problems you are facing.

The first step is to learn how to cope with the physical symptoms of stress. These could be a tightening feeling in the stomach, feeling nervous, having sweaty palms, headaches, etc. We have included a selection of deep breathing and relaxation exercises in this book in *Chapter Eight – Activities to enhance your well-being* to help you manage the negative stress and anxiety.

The second step is to learn how to cope with the psychological reactions. To do this, you need to uncover what prickly thoughts may be causing you to feel anxious. If you are feeling excessive anxiety this could be due to your particular style of thinking.

Catastrophizing, whereby you think in a way that magnifies a bad experience out of proportion to its actual likely consequence is a common source of anxiety. Here are some examples: *"I couldn't help the children with their homework, so they'll never succeed at school"* or, *"She didn't want to make love to me, so that means she's thinking of leaving me."* In some cases, anxious feelings are due to always expecting everything to be bad all the time, because of one experience: *"He didn't like what I cooked tonight. This means I am a useless cook and no one will ever like what I cook ever again."*

In each case, the person thinking these thoughts will feel tremendous levels of anxiety, because they think that their experiences will result in devastating and far-reaching, negative consequences.

Coping with anxiety involves the same techniques that we discussed earlier in the book when we talked about dealing with prickly thoughts. It can be so helpful for you to challenge the thoughts that are causing your anxiety. Look at the event and become aware of your filters. Prepare your action plan, accordingly. This process will help you to replace your prickly thoughts with more helpful thoughts. For example, if your partner did not want to make love one night and your thoughts tell you that she does not love you anymore, counter that by saying, *"Wait a minute. Is that really true? She didn't want to make love, but she is here with me and showing me she cares for me."*

When we challenge prickly thoughts, it opens up the way to replace them with far more realistic ones. You could then go on to consider that perhaps she was tired and she knew she had an early start the next day so she wanted to rest. You can now see that your partner does indeed still love and care for you and that there were reasonable and practical reasons for her response.

If you cannot think of a thought to replace the first one, you could ask yourself what the advantages and disadvantages are in thinking the way you are thinking. If you examine your prickly thought in a rational manner, you will be able to see that there is probably a different way of thinking about the event and that there are no advantages in thinking the way you were thinking initially. You will then see that the situation is not as bad as you originally thought. So, using the example above, if you had thought that your partner no longer loved you, because she did not want to make love that night, you could ask yourself what the advantages are in thinking that way. When you realize that there are no advantages to your way of thinking, you might be able to consider other lines of thought.

As you replace your prickly thoughts with thoughts that are more rational, you will be able to move on. If you experience difficulty with this process, ask your partner to help you. You could always also check out the reality of a particular thought by asking your partner how they really felt. Be mindful to use a constructive language when you do this. Use the worksheets together and help each other through the process.

Sometimes, in moments of high anxiety, you can also use distraction techniques as a way of coping. Try to focus your mind on something else, something that can relax you. For instance, you can practice your deep breathing and relaxation exercises. There are countless mental and physical activities you can do, depending on the time of day and where you are. This might be easier to achieve if you physically remove yourself from the situation that has been distressing you. Once you start to feel relaxed, you will be able to challenge your prickly thoughts as we discussed earlier.

Distraction techniques can vary from person to person and for each situation. Here is a selection of techniques that many people find helpful:

> *Deep breathing or focusing on counting the number of breaths you take.*

> *Listen to music, read a magazine or do something focused like cross-stitch.*

> *Engage in mental puzzles like crosswords, word searches or sudoku.*

> *Tidy up the house, organize your closet, do a little gardening.*

> *Take a walk, go for a bicycle ride or play a sport.*

Remember, the key here is to do something that you find relaxing. Choose something that you can do easily and that allows you to focus your mind quickly.

If you know that you are prone to feeling stress and anxiety, especially in certain types of situations or events, get to know your baseline so that you know what you can cope with as we explained in *Chapter Three – Assessing the situation*. Identify for yourself what you need to do to de-stress and feel calm again.

Also, every time you manage your stress and anxiety, remember to give yourself a mental *"well done!"* This positive validation completes the process of replacing the prickly thoughts and feelings that caused stress and anxiety with your realistic, rational and practical thoughts.

Depression

Depression can manifest itself in different ways. Generally speaking, people who are depressed say that they are feeling *"down"* or that they *"do not feel like doing anything"*. Some familiar symptoms are lack of motivation, loss of appetite, not sleeping well, loss of interest in the various aspects of your life or the world around you and feeling excessively emotional or tearful.

There is a difference between depression and mood swings. Feeling low can sometimes be construed as feeling depressed, but this does not necessarily mean that you are suffering from depression. Depression usually involves feeling consistently low and tearful over a long period of time. Mood swings, on the other hand, involve a fluctuation of feelings. You may feel excited for a while and then feel low for a while. Mood swings are explained in further detail later in this chapter.

Severe depression is something that requires professional help. If you feel extreme negative emotions and feelings, a complete lack of motivation to the point where you cannot get out of bed in the morning, or you are not able to take part in your normal life routine or activities, please consult your doctor for further help.

However, many people often say they are depressed when, in fact, they feel low or sad due to a situation in which they find themselves or due to an adverse event they have experienced. If that is the case, working through the worksheets will help you to address the issues you are facing. In *Chapter Five – How to use the worksheets to help you through the process*, we discussed John and Tara's situation and how they used the worksheets to address the issues that they were facing.

Whatever the causes of the symptoms you are experiencing, you can help yourself to some extent by following this simple plan:

> *Eat healthy foods at regular mealtimes.*

> *Avoid too much sugar, snacks and fast foods. Establish a regular time to go to bed, preferably before eleven o'clock in the evening and allow yourself eight hours' sleep.*

> *Do some exercise at regular times throughout the week.*

> *Relax – look at our relaxation exercises.*

> *Try and think of one positive thought for the day that brings a smile to your face.*

Working through issues

Grief

As with all emotions, grief is very much a part of life. We all experience it, sometimes to a lesser or greater degree, throughout our lives. Usually, we feel grief due to a significant loss. We may feel grief at the death of a much-loved family member or a pet who has been a constant companion. We may feel grief when we are separated for long periods from someone we love in life.

We learn, through experience, what grief is and how we respond to it. We all respond differently to situations. Some people may feel intense sadness the moment they learn of someone's death. Another person may feel numb for some time before feelings of grief set in. Sometimes, even the thought of someone close to us dying may produce feelings of grief. Furthermore, we all show our grief in different ways. Some of us may cry immediately, some of us much later on. Sometimes, people act out of character and may withdraw into themselves. Others may remain calm and take up a practical role for themselves. Yet others may feel themselves getting more irritated and agitated, when really underneath they are feeling sadness and grief.

The important thing is to be nonjudgmental about ourselves or others when undergoing a grieving process. For most of us, talking about how we feel and what we think, helps us to accept the process of grief that we are going through. It also helps us to understand the distress that we feel: the loss we feel in the present, as well as, what we might expect to feel in the future. Once we understand what it is we are feeling, we are better able to help ourselves and our family. By going through this process, our levels of distress can start to come down and eventually, allow us to move on with our lives.

Sometimes, we feel we have worked through our grief when it suddenly catches us by surprise. We might find ourselves suddenly tearful when we are reminded of the person we have lost, even if it was a long time ago. This is quite common, especially during anniversaries or the holidays. If this occurs, it is important not to criticize yourself for having these feelings or thoughts. It can also be very healing to allow yourself to cry. Try to acknowledge your thoughts and feelings and allow yourself to feel whatever it is you feel. This may also help you to remember the times you shared with the person for whom you are grieving.

If you and/or your partner are finding it difficult to go through the grieving process, it may be helpful to sit down and work through the worksheets together. Sometimes, it is difficult to know where to begin to talk and writing down your thoughts and feelings is a good place to start. It may also help you to identify any negative feelings or prickly thoughts that may be recurring during this process, which may be impeding your ability to work through your feelings about the event.

It may be that you feel that you need more help than we can provide within the context of this book with your grieving process.

Should this be the case, please contact your doctor, who can help you access professional help.

Anger, frustration and irritability

Anger, frustration and irritability are emotions that we all experience from time to time. For example, we may feel quite angry if someone has acted unjustly towards us or we may feel irritated if we are in a hurry and we are kept on hold on the telephone for a very long time. It is usually healthy to express our emotions and feelings as long as they are expressed in a controlled way so that we are not hurtful to ourselves or to others.

Communication is the key to keeping our levels of anger and frustration under control. It is healthy to talk about how we feel in a given situation. Sometimes, if we deny our feelings of frustration or try to bottle them up, it can result in angry outbursts at a future date. When this happens, it can produce high levels of anxiety in us, as well as, in our family. Try and remember the example of how John and Tara dealt with the emotions. John's angry outbursts distressed his partner, because they were unpredictable and seemingly unrelated to anything that was happening at the moment. Obviously, this was not a healthy way to express how he was feeling or what he was thinking.

If you know that certain situations make you feel irritated, you can prepare yourself for your responses. For example, you may feel very irritated by the way a friend eats. If you cannot or do not wish to avoid eating with them, then plan for this event. Perhaps you need to practice some slow breathing when you feel your level of irritation rise or use a distraction technique like listening to somebody's conversation. You could also try and understand why you are feeling so irritated about their manner of eating. Maybe it triggers something in you that relates to some other experiences, which you encountered in the past. After all, it shouldn't really bother you, because it is your friend's problem and not yours.

Sometimes, we feel angry and irritated over events from our past experiences. Sometimes, as in Lydia's example, the anger comes from our own filters, the unrealistic assumptions or prickly thoughts that we have about ourselves. In a relationship, it is also important to consider that anger can also come about from the way two people interact with each other.

In a relationship, we have rules about how we behave with each, how we live our lives together and how we choose to interact with others outside of the relationship. It is very common for people to feel angry or frustrated when rules are broken within a relationship. Breaking rules can have a physical, psychological or financial consequence. For example, you may have a rule in your home that when people play ball in the garden they must use a soft ball. If someone uses a hard ball, instead, and breaks a window, the broken glass may injure someone and there will be the cost of replacing the window. In this case, your anger will have been triggered by what you perceive as someone deciding to go against the rules. There are many potential consequences, as a result of a rule not being adhered to.

At other times, there is an emotional cost to breaking rules. The most obvious one is if you and your partner have an agreement to be faithful to each other and one person decides to see someone else. Usually, there is not only a great deal of anger, but the trust between the two partners can break down and this becomes a complex issue. A less dramatic scenario is when one partner feels angry, because they feel that the other has stepped beyond the boundaries of their relationship. For example, if you and your partner decide to keep certain things private between the two of you and then one of you goes off and discusses these things with someone else, it violates the agreement that you have with each other. Even contradicting each other in front of others in a casual conversation can cause a lot of emotional fall-out if the argument that follows is bad enough. Your partner may not feel backed up and supported by you.

Whatever may be causing the feelings of anger, irritability or frustration you are experiencing, use the worksheets provided here in this book to identify and work through them. Work on your relaxation, deep breathing, mindfulness and distraction techniques to help you manage and cope with difficult events. The more you learn to produce constructive responses to events, the more you will produce positive outcomes, instead of prickly thoughts and distressing consequences for yourselves.

Again, if you feel you need professional help, please contact your doctor to access the appropriate services.

Anger can take on many forms. In the event that domestic violence is involved, you MUST seek help from outside sources. Violence against one partner, each other or your children is absolutely not acceptable. Please do not ever try to convince yourself that it is *"not so bad"* or that *"I/he/she/they deserved it."* It is never ever justified and it is against the law. Before you can begin to work on the difficulties in your relationship, it is paramount that the violent partner or partners seek help from a professional source. It is simply not feasible to try to work together on solving the issues present in your relationship unless both partners feel safe. For information on what to do, where to go and what resources are available, please contact your doctor, the Citizen's Advice Bureau and/or your local police authority or ring the Domestic Violence Helpline.

Jealousy

Feeling 'jealous' can be a common feeling when you are in a relationship. You might feel a little envious of your partner if they receive a promotion at work. Equally your partner may feel a little jealous of you if you are presented with the opportunity to have a fabulous holiday with your friends, while they have to go to work. On the whole, this sort of jealousy is not threatening to the relationship as long as you recognize that it is simply an ordinary response to feeling a little left out and do not feel any need to act on it. We might call this 'non-prickly' jealousy, because it is short-lived and soon replaced by feeling happy and supportive of your partner's good fortune. In these situations, it usually helps if you openly acknowledge to your partner that you have these feelings. Once you do, you will probably both be able to laugh about it and share in the joy that something good has happened to your partner.

Jealousy can be problematic, however, when it goes beyond these boundaries. Jealousy in its true form is when someone feels very suspicious and/or angry about some perceived rivalry. For example, if the feelings of jealousy over your partner's promotion persists and you find yourself inventing and reacting to a series of irrational thoughts, you will not be able to feel supportive of them. This type of jealousy can be called 'prickly' jealousy, because the feelings you are experiencing link to the assumptions and prickly thoughts you are having about your partner and the event. You will need to work on your prickly thoughts and how they are affecting your relationship before you can progress together in a positive way.

Here is a common example of prickly jealousy. Imagine that you and your partner are having a drink together at a bar. You leave for a few minutes and when you return, you see your partner is talking to an attractive person. You may immediately think that your partner is flirting and that they are more interested in that person than they are in you. You might also think that the other person wants to take your partner away from you. Your next thought is that your partner is more attracted to this person and that they want to end the relationship with you. Before you know it, you are thinking that there is no future in your relationship together and you ask your partner to leave the bar with you. You may then after you have left give your partner a very hard time for having talked to the attractive person and this might lead to a painful argument between the two of you. Your partner may be very hurt by this, because as far as they are concerned they had planned to spend a nice evening with you.

As you can see in the above example, this series of irrational thoughts caused you to react irrationally and unfairly to your partner. Moreover, you gave your partner no opportunity to introduce the other person or explain the event. Perhaps it was someone your partner works with who happened to be there and they were having a friendly chat. Or, your partner may have been approached by this other person and was simply being polite to them until you returned.

Let's take the same scenario and play it out along more rational lines. When you return and see your partner talking to this person, you join them and behave in a civil manner. A prickly jealous thought comes to your mind, but you do not allow it to control your thoughts or actions. Instead, you wait for an appropriate moment to discuss the event with your partner. Equally, you may find out that the other person is really very nice and that they have no intentions, whatsoever, to get in the way of your partner and yourself and that there is no reason to feel any jealousy at all.

This course of action will help prevent you from getting caught up in a spiral of irrational thoughts and actions and prickly jealousy. Instead of ruining and curtailing the good time you were having together, as in the first example, your decision not to allow the prickly thoughts to take over and rush you into immediate action, along with the quick conversation with your partner or your own discovery about the nature of the interaction with this person, helped put to rest the jealous thoughts that you were having.

When 'prickly' jealousy occurs and you find yourself thinking irrationally, work through your thoughts using *Worksheet One*. When you work through the worksheets you will come to a better understanding of your thought process, as well as, a better understanding of your partner. Go through *Worksheet Two* to establish the 'baseline' in your relationship for trusting each other. By doing so, your anxieties regarding your relationship with your partner will be reduced. Instead of feeling threatened by your partner interacting with other people, progressing in their career, developing new interests, etc., you will be able to enjoy each other more fully.

Your sexual relationship

Physical and emotional desire for each other plays a significant role in a couple's relationship. Your sexual relationship with your partner involves a lot more than straightforward sex. It is about you and your partner's desire and need for each other's physical touch, as well as, emotional closeness and intimacy.

As with any aspect of your relationship, in order to feel completely at ease and open with your partner, you need to be able to communicate your needs and feelings with each other. You may find it difficult to talk about sex – whether this concerns your own needs or your partner's – if you are not used to doing so. This is not uncommon, but it is something that you can learn. So please do not feel disheartened. Explain to your partner that you feel shy. It can be helpful for you to start by discussing positive experiences, before moving on to the issue you would like to discuss.

For example, you might say: *"I really like it when you kiss me"*, before you tell your partner that *"I would really like to try such-and-such,"* or *"I'm not so comfortable with such-and-such."*

It is helpful to be specific about what you would like or do not like, so that you do not end up making assumptions about what the other is trying to say. Likewise, neither person should ever assume that the other should know what they want. Ask gentle questions for clarification and always remain open and compassionate towards each other. Just like in any other area of your relationship, if there is a conflict, talk about it and negotiate with each other. This will reduce any resentment you may be feeling and help you to clear up any problems that have arisen.

Perhaps the most common area of conflict in a couple's sexual relationship is when one partner wants to have sex and the other does not. In most cases, there is usually a short-term reason for not being in the mood. For example, you may be feeling very romantic and sexy, but your partner may not. Have a talk about it. It may be that your partner is feeling too stressed to be in the mood for sex, because it is six-thirty in the morning and if they had sex with you they would be late for work. Or perhaps it is a quarter to midnight and they are feeling tired and exhausted after a very hard day. At other times, they might simply need a little time to unwind at the end of the day, before feeling in the mood for sexual closeness. Each partner needs to understand how the other is feeling and both partners need to be flexible at the same time.

Sometimes, after an argument, one partner wants to have sex right away and the other does not. Again, talk about this and respect each other's feelings in this situation. The partner who wants to have sex may feel they need to reaffirm how they feel for each other. The other partner may need a little more time to let go of all the negative feelings they have been experiencing.

If one partner never wants to have sex and consistently goes to great effort to avoid it, it may be helpful for you both to discuss this issue with your doctor. There may be a serious underlying physical or psychological reason, which needs to be addressed.

Another common problem that many couples experience is not having enough time for a good sexual relationship. We all lead very busy lives and sometimes it is difficult to be in the mood when there is so much that demands our time. Again, it is important to talk about this so that you both understand that it is not through lack of desire that you have not had sex. It may be helpful and rather fun for your relationship to plan ahead. Perhaps you decide that Wednesday nights will be your night for sex. That way, you can plan your week so that you are home by a reasonable time with no or few commitments on Wednesday evenings. You can give yourselves time to unwind and talk together so that you feel relaxed. If you feel that sex ought to be more spontaneous than this, ask yourselves how often you have been able to be spontaneous about it in recent months. If the answer is rarely, give this system a try. It can create a sense of fun and anticipation that may surprise you.

Sometimes, sex becomes an issue for a couple, because one or both partners feel they have not achieved a certain level of physical enjoyment or satisfaction. First and foremost, please try not to judge yourself or your partner and do not criticize each other. Use this as a learning process rather than feel pressurized about it. Try to understand what expectations you and/or your partner may have and whether these are realistic. Talk and listen to each other about what is pleasurable. What is enjoyable and exciting for one person is not necessarily so for another. Women in particular may find that their bodies are more sensitive at certain times than at others so it is important to communicate this.

In this context also, you might find it helpful to use the worksheets to understand what was or was not successful. Make a list of suggestions on how to make it better and more enjoyable the next time. Most importantly, remain relaxed and flexible about your experience. Like any experience in life, there is a range in sexual enjoyment. Sometimes it might be 'fair to moderate' and at other times it is 'excellent.' There are many physical and emotional factors that influence your experience, such as, how you feel, your stress levels, what's on your mind and whether you feel under the weather and lethargic or fit, healthy and attractive.

A couple's sexual relationship is not just about how often or how well they have sex. It is about how comfortable they feel with each other physically and emotionally. Sometimes, the most satisfying experience is to hug each other and know that your partner is the one person with whom you can share your thoughts and heart. To achieve this level of intimacy, this can go beyond your sex life. It involves how you treat each other every day in public and in private. Do you speak to each other with love and respect? Do you honor each other's trust? Do you behave in a way that shows your regard for your partner? Are loving words and gestures, showing physical affection and appreciation for each other, part of your daily lives? If any of your answers is a *"no,"* you might like to start to think about what you could do differently in order to show you appreciate each other.

Finally, remember to show that you desire each other however long you may have been together. There are significant times in your lives when you may need some extra reassurance that you are still loved and still desired. When your children leave home to start their own lives, you may feel that your roles are no longer the same and it may take some time for you to see yourselves in this new light. Retirement from work is also a time when people usually re-evaluate their role in life. Also, as we grow older, we all experience changes in our bodies, which may make us feel different and make us aware that we are entering a new stage. Although each new stage in life is something to look forward to, each phase also represents times of change during which we can all use some extra support and affirmation about our place in our relationships. This is especially important if your relationship involves times of prolonged or repeated illness of a partner.

If you feel that you need more help than can be offered within the context of this book, please contact your doctor to be referred to the appropriate professional services in your area.

Mood swings

We all experience a variety of moods throughout the day. For example, you may wake up feeling tired and the thought of having to face a hard day at work might make you feel a little down. Then, you have a very good morning at work and you feel quite happy. On your way home, perhaps someone is rude to you and you feel a bit annoyed. When you get home, you find that your partner has already started to cook dinner and you feel delighted and pleased to be home.

Feeling a range of emotions in moderation is perfectly normal. However, perhaps you find that your mood goes up and down frequently. If there are regular changes within a short period of time between sudden feelings of positive emotions (for example, excitement or joy) and sudden feelings of negative emotions (for example, feeling sad or angry) it is likely that you are suffering from mood swings. Most probably, these fluctuations will have some effect on your relationship with your partner and on other people around you. To handle your mood swings, be mindful about how you are feeling. It is also helpful to try and communicate with your partner about your situation.

Mood swings can happen for a variety of reasons and if they persist, it is a good idea to consult your doctor, especially if you feel extreme negative emotions and feelings intensely or for long periods of time. Sometimes, there might be an underlying physical cause. For example, mood swings can occur due to hormonal imbalances, illnesses, such as, diabetes, or even as a reaction to any medication you may be taking.

It is helpful for both you and your partner to know when these mood swings occur, since this may help you to identify the cause. For example, if you suddenly find yourself feeling low and lethargic, try to determine what may have triggered this feeling. Perhaps something specific happened just before you felt this way. Or, you may have neglected to eat for too long during the day. Keep a record of these episodes. You may find that there is a relationship between events and your moods. For example, if you find your moods are stress related, make adjustments to minimize your stress levels and learn to cope with the stress you experience. If your moods are related to physical reasons, make adjustments to overcome them. For example, you may find you need to exercise or eat more regularly, cut out sugary foods or develop a healthier lifestyle.

Sometimes, you may find that you experience these moods but that you cannot find a consistent cause for them. Discuss this with your partner and explain what you are experiencing. If you have thought of some ways to help yourself, talk about these as well. Be open to suggestions and accept them if you feel they make sense to you and seem reasonable and that it is something you can actually do for yourself.

In addition to writing down your moods when they occur and trying to determine if there is a trigger for them, it may be helpful to rate your moods. Use a scale of one to ten (ten being the highest rating and one the lowest) to monitor your moods.

This will help you to differentiate between a normal reaction to an event (a rating of up to five) and an irrational, intense reaction (ratings between six and ten). You can use this information to prioritize the moods you feel you need to work on and write an action plan to help you with this. Even if you find that most of your feelings are well over six on the scale, you can still use this system to identify your moods and decide what you want to work on first.

Here are some strategies you can use to help you cope with your moods:

> *Be aware of your moods, especially when they catch your attention. Write them down and rate them so that you begin to get an idea of when (and possibly why) they occur.*

> *Plan an activity that you can look forward to each day. This may perhaps involve spending a little time with the children or taking your dog for a walk. Allocate some relaxation time with your partner.*

> *Exercise plays a significant role in managing your moods. When you exercise, your energy level increases and uplifts your mood. Exercise also boosts the serotonin levels in your brain, which produces happy feelings. However, try a balanced approach to exercising rather than using it to excess.*

> *Be aware of your diet. Eat healthily. Cut down on sugar in your snacks and drinks; refined sugar can cause your moods*

and energy levels to go up and down abruptly. Cut down on caffeine, which can also affect moods. Reduce or cut out alcohol, because alcohol acts as a depressant on our brain and if you are prone to feeling down, it may intensify that mood. Try to eat well-balanced meals, avoiding artificial colouring, preservatives and transfats, as much as possible. Studies have shown that food additives can affect moods, making us hyperactive, for example.

> Improve the quality of your sleep. Try to avoid caffeine after six o'clock in the evening and do not eat a heavy meal just before you go to bed. Have a warm bath, if you like, but make sure it is not too hot. A too hot bath can overstimulate your senses and make it difficult for you to fall asleep. You could also use some relaxing aromatherapy oils, such as lavender, in your bath.

> Make your bedroom into a peaceful place to sleep. It is not helpful to have a television or computer in there. Stop using the computer or watching television at least half an hour before going to bed. This will allow your brain to switch off from the stimulation it has had. Try not to smoke in your bedroom if you smoke. Open a window at night (safety permitting) to keep the air in your bedroom fresh and clean, or open the ventilation in your window. You may also check your bedroom for anything else that does not feel calming to you, such as the colours of the walls or the pictures that you have in the bedroom or too many things in your bedroom.

> Change your lifestyle in whatever way you can to reduce stress levels. Create a relaxing environment for yourself and your family. This may take some organization and planning, but it will be well worth it for everyone.

> Use the mindfulness exercise to relax. You can even use it as a distraction exercise when you are suffering from a mood. Being mindful will give you more insight into your situation. It will enable you to center yourself, which in turn, helps you to focus better.

> Be mindful of your environment and create a pleasant place. Listen to uplifting music, read entertaining books, watch upbeat movies.

> Make some time for yourself and your interests. This could be something new or something you used to do. It is important that you feel comfortable emotionally and financially with what you do, but do something for yourself that interests you.

> Use the worksheets we have discussed throughout this book to help you work on your issues. Once you can understand your prickly thoughts from a different perspective, you will be able to see that the situation is often not as bad as you initially thought. This realization will help you to start transforming your prickly thoughts into more rational, positive and soothing thoughts, which in turn, will have a positive effect on your overall mood.

Medical conditions

If you and/or your partner have medical conditions involving physical problems, it is important that you discuss this with the relevant medical professional. In the first instance, it is important that you have an accurate diagnosis of the condition. More specifically, you need to know what you can do about it. It is also important that you are clear about how your medical condition may affect your daily life. If the physical condition limits you in any way or causes you to take special measures, it is especially important that you discuss this together with your partner so that both of you understand what adjustments you may need to make together.

Sometimes the problems may be short-term and these are relatively easy to deal with, because you know the situation will change and revert back to normal. Perhaps one of you is recovering from a broken leg and unable to drive. In most cases, your doctor will be able to give you a timeframe for healing so that you can plan your life accordingly. Put together an action plan to include the necessary adjustments you will need to make until you are able to drive again.

Another common short-term condition that may require some adjustment for couples is pregnancy. Even with perfectly healthy pregnancies, many women experience times when they feel unwell or tired. Have a discussion about how you will cope together as a couple and adjust your daily lives accordingly. You might also find it really helpful to attend parenting classes together, especially if you are new parents.

In the busy lives we lead today, it is all too easy to look upon physical conditions as inconveniences. Both the person undergoing these conditions and their partner may feel annoyed that they have to make adjustments for the condition. It is particularly important to be aware of your thought process through this time and to remain flexible and compassionate. This is especially true when dealing with long-term conditions. One of the most stressful aspects of a long-term condition is that we do not necessarily know what the outcome might be. Long-term conditions can be everything from chronic back pain to being treated for cancer. It might be impotency or living with illness, it could be coping with a partner who is exhibiting signs of Alzheimer or someone who is losing their hearing.

If you and your partner have to cope with a long-term condition, it is important that you speak to your medical professional so that you can understand the prognosis. You may also find it helpful to research the condition to expand your understanding of it. There are also many excellent support groups for various conditions and it is worthwhile contacting them. Generally speaking, long-term conditions require long-term adjustments to your life together. You may find that you need extra help in order to help you cope and this is nothing to be ashamed of. Contact your medical professional, social services, your community organizations, voluntary services and your friends and family. There are many support groups for sufferers of particular conditions and their partners or family, which may be of good help.

When a partner dies

A couple's relationship with each other does not necessarily end even if one partner dies. At first, of course, the sense of loss can be very acute. You may feel – your partner's absence constantly and it can be a very painful process to come to terms with your partner's death.

Many people who have lost their partners say that after they have gone through the initial grieving process, they feel that their 'relationship' with their partner moves into a new phase. Their partner is no longer with them physically, but they become aware of how much their partner was a part of their lives. When you have thoughts or feelings like this about your deceased partner, they may overwhelm you. Allow yourself to remember the good times you had together and make a memory diary if you wish. This activity may be soothing and therapeutic in helping you come to terms with and adjust to your new life.

New routines when it happens

Life without your partner can involve many practical adjustments for you (as well as) your family and friends). It is quite common that in many partnerships, each partner has specific jobs as part of his or her role. For example, one person may do most of the cooking and shopping, while another takes care of the garden. One person may be responsible for the accounts, while another takes care of the car and so on. Suddenly, you may find having to take on the tasks your partner used to do. This may feel overwhelming at first, but it can be done. Write down an on-going list of what needs to be done. This will help you to prioritize what you need to do and put together an action plan for yourself.

You may also experience many emotional adjustments to your life without your partner. If you were the primary caregiver to a partner who was ill for a prolonged period of time, you may feel initially that you have no role. You may also experience very mixed feelings. For example, you may feel quite relieved that your ill partner has been released from the suffering but you may also find yourself wishing that they were still there. These feelings may seem contradictory, but they are perfectly normal. It means that you are missing them deeply and that you are grieving their loss. Even if you were not the primary caregiver, many people who lose their partners feel they have to create a new role for themselves. Some people say that they became aware of just how much they identified with being one part of a couple.

After a period of time, you may feel you would like to bring a new person into your life. Your family and friends may be very supportive of your decision. However, sometimes, difficulties with your family and friends may arise over decisions you take for yourself. For example, your children (even if they are well into adulthood) may feel upset should you decide to take a new partner. Please try to remember that while they may have your best interests at heart, only you can make decisions regarding your life and how you choose to live it.

There may be many different factors to consider involving a new relationship. Keep your thinking rational and create an action plan of 'how and when'. Creating and following an action plan will then help you to feel more confident about planning for the future.

If at any time you find the whole experience really too difficult to cope with, it could be very helpful for you to talk it through with your doctor for further advice.

Resistance to change

One obstacle you may encounter when you start trying to make changes can be a resistance to change. While you and your partner may wish to improve your relationship, one or both of you may find it difficult to cope with changes to your established way of doing things. If you do encounter resistance to change, it may be necessary to look at the possible reasons behind it.

People resist change for various reasons. Some people may feel that they might lose something of value or they misunderstand what the change involves or implies. Others may not believe the change makes sense or they may have a low tolerance for change. Assessing the possible reasons for resistance to change can help you and your partner to select the appropriate ways to overcome it. Take a look at the section on strengths and opportunities as explained in *Chapter Three – Assessing the situation*. This will help you to work on any resistance to change you or your partner may be experiencing.

Bringing about changes in one's practical life is similar to learning to change behaviour. You need to assess what the situation is, your thoughts and emotions about it and the possible outcomes if a change is implemented. The most essential factor in overcoming resistance is communication, negotiation and education. Sometimes it becomes essential to help each other see the possible positive outcomes for changing the way you organize your practical life.

chapter ten

The way forward

Well, now that you have reached the final chapter of this book, you can congratulate yourselves that you have come a long way!

In Part I, we introduced you to the importance of understanding the event and the underlying issues that are presenting difficulties in your relationship. We encouraged you to uncover and understand what your beliefs are regarding your relationship and to identify your prickly thoughts, which produce negative emotions and feelings in you.

We also encouraged you to identify your strengths and the opportunities in your relationship and highlighted ways of helping you work on change, such as, deciding on an action plan for both of you to follow. We also talked about how to achieve your goals, communicate effectively and stay focused. We presented techniques on how to relax and be mindful about the whole process of making your relationship better and bringing about changes.

In Part II of this book, we included a section on the importance of eating healthily and sleeping well. We would like to encourage you to continue to try and use deep breathing regularly and to do at least one activity mindfully each day. Regard this as time you give to yourself!

Finally, we gave you an overview of common issues that may be present when couples have difficulties within their relationship. We hope that this information may be useful in helping you understand your situation better so that the difficulties you are experiencing may be resolved.

While you may have chosen to read and work through this book to help you with a specific difficulty, you can use the techniques we have presented again and again to help you to work through any other issues that may come up. Ideally, we hope that you will choose to incorporate many of these skills into your daily lives so that they become second nature to you.

As we have stated throughout the book, if, at any time, however, you feel you are really struggling with a particular issue or situation and feel that you cannot work through it, please ask for professional help. We provide you with a list of useful contacts in *Appendix Two*.

This ending is simply the beginning. We sincerely hope that, through the exercises and the skills we have presented, you have gained a better understanding of yourselves and your situation and have been able to see your way forward. We now encourage you to use these newly learned techniques in your daily life and interactions as an individual and together as a couple so that you can create for yourselves the truly fulfilling relationship you deserve.

We wish you the very best on your journey.

Appendices

Appendix I

Further Reading

The Feeling Good Handbook, by David D. Burns, Penguin Books Ltd., 1990.

Overcoming Anger and Irritability: A Self-help Guide using Cognitive Behavioural Techniques, by William Davies, Constable & Robinson, 2000.

The Anger Workbook for Women: How to Keep your Anger from Undermining your Self Esteem, your Emotional Balance, and your Relationships, by Laura J. Petracek, Publisher, 2004.

Managing Anxiety, A training manual, by Helen Kennedy, Oxford Medical Publications, 1990.

Overcoming Anxiety, A Self-help Guide using Cognitive Behavioural Techniques, by Helen Kennerley, Constable & Robinson, 1997.

You Must Relax, by E. Jacobsen, Souvenir Press, 1976.

Love is Never Enough, by A. Beck, Penguin, 1988.

Therapy with Couples, by M. Crowe, and J. Ridley, Blackwell, 1990.

Do You Feel Loved by Me?, by Philip Rogers, Living Well, 1998.

How to Love and be Loved, by Dr. Paul Hauck, Sheldon Press, 1997.

Wherever you go, there you are: Mindfulness Meditation in Everyday life, by J. Kabat –Zinn, Hyperion, 1994.

Coming to Our Senses: Healing Ourselves and the World Through Mindfulness, by Jon Kabat-Zinn, Piatkus, 2005

The Miracle of Mindfulness, The Classic Guide to Meditation by the World's Most Revered Master, by Thich Nhat Hanh, Rider, 2008

The Power of Now, by Eckhart Tolle, Penguin, 1997

*All these titles and many more you can easily order via our online bookshop at **www.oxdev.co.uk***

Appendix II

Where to go for further help

You may feel that you or your partner need to work on personal issues before being able to start working on your relationship difficulties. If this is the case, visit your doctor and discuss your needs. They may be able to refer you and/or your partner to various services that are helpful in addressing your needs. They may also provide you with advice on an appropriate course of action based on your circumstances.

You can also ask to see a counsellor at the GP's surgery. If this person is trained to see couples, then you may be able to be seen within the GP surgery. They may also be able to offer support while you are waiting to be seen by other specialist services. ""They may suggest that you contact your local branch of Relate, various other community-counseling services or a private relationship counsellor, a Chartered Clinical Psychologist or a specialist psychotherapist, such as a Cognitive Behavioural Psychotherapist or a Systemic Psychotherapist. If your doctor is unable to identify a suitable professional to help you, you could also look for a private psychotherapist or a Chartered Clinical Psychologist.

The British Psychological Society (BPS), the British Association for Behavioural and Cognitive Psychotherapies (BABCP) and The United Kingdom Council for Psychotherapy (UKCP) all have registers of their qualified and accredited professionals. You will find their contact details, below. If you choose to utilize the help of a private professional ensure that they are sufficiently trained and that they are registered with and endorsed by a Professional Association.

Useful Contacts

Relate National Marriage Guidance
Tel: 01788 573 241 Fax: 01788 535 007
Relate is a registered charity with 108 centres in England and Wales.

Relate Northern Ireland, Belfast
Tel: 01232323454   Fax: 01232 315298

British Association for Behavioural and Cognitive Psychotherapies (BABCP)
Tel: +44 (0) 1617 974 484   Fax: +44 (0) 1617 972 670
e-mail: babcp@babcp.com   web: www.babcp.com

The British Psychological Society (BPS)
Tel: +44 (0)116 254 9568   Fax: +44 (0)116 227 1314
E-mail: enquiries@bps.org.uk   web: www.bps.org.uk

CRUSE Bereavement Care
Tel: 020 8940 4818   Helpline 0870 1671677
Cruise Bereavement Care provides Counselling in 180 branches

Centre for Stress Management
Tel: 020 8318 4448   Web: www.managingstress.com
A private, independent service for stress management

Depression Alliance
Tel: 0845 123 23 20

Medical Advisory Service, General Medical Helpline
Tel: 020 8994 9874

NHS Direct
Tel: 0845 46 47   Web: www.direct.nhs.uk

National Centre for Domestic Violence
Tel: 08709 220704 *(24 Hrs a day and 365 days a year.)*

National domestic violence helpline
Tel: 0808 2000 247

Oxfordshire's Independent Psychology Service
47 High Street, Witney, Oxfordshire, OX28 6JA
Tel: 01993 77 99 94   email: indpsy@oxdev.co.uk
web: www.oxdev.co.uk
Oxfordshire's longest established, private psychological therapy service, offering individually tailored assessments and therapy for a wide range of psychological problems, including partner and family therapy. The focus is on empowerment, well-being and health.

Samaritans
Tel: 08457 909090 (UK) & 1850 609 090 (Ireland)
Web: www.samaritans.org.uk
Offers support 24 hours a day in 203 centres

Saneline
Tel: 0845 767 8000

The Oxford Stress and Trauma Centre
47 High Street, Witney, Oxfordshire, OX28 6JA
Tel: 01993 77 90 77   e-mail: stress.trauma@oxdev.co.uk
Web: www.oxdev.co.uk
Oxfordshire's longest established private, specialist service for trauma and stress-related problems, including experiences of abuse and violence.

United Kingdom Council for Psychotherapy (UKCP)
Tel: +44 (0) 20 70149955   Fax: +44 (0) 20 7014 9977
E-mail: info@psychotherapy.org.uk
Web: www.psychotherapy.org.uk

Appendix III

THE EVENT
What's happened?

How we BEHAVE,
based on how we feel
and what we think

Model One

OUR FILTERS
How we interpret
the event

How we FEEL
about the
event

What we THINK
about the event

Partner A & Partner B
THE EVENT
What's
happened?

Partner A
MY FILTERS
How I interpret
the event

Partner B
MY FILTERS
How I interpret
the event

What I THINK
about the event

What I THINK
about the event

Model Two

How I FEEL about
the event. What
are my emotions?

How I FEEL about
the event. What
are my emotions?

How I BEHAVE,
based on how I feel
and what I think

How I BEHAVE,
based on how I feel
and what I think

What IMPACT did
our actions have on
our relationship?

Mr & Mrs A
THE EVENT
What's happened?

Mr A
MY FILTERS
How I interpret
the event

What IMPACT did our
actions have on our
relationship?

Mrs A
MY FILTERS
How I interpret
the event

How we BEHAVE,
based on how we feel
and what we think

Communicate
& negotiate use
WORKSHEETS 1, 2, 3

Model Three

How we FEEL.
What are our
emotions?

Mr & Mrs A
OUR FILTERS
How we interpret the
event

What we THINK
about the event

Appendix IV

WORKSHEET ONE
UNDERSTANDING WHAT HAPPENED

NAME	
EVENT	
PRICKLY THOUGHTS	
EMOTIONS & FEELINGS	
RATING	
WHAT I WANT TO CHANGE	

WORKSHEET TWO
WHAT WE ARE GOING TO DO

EVENT		
NAME		
REACTION		
WHAT WE WANT TO CHANGE		

WORKSHEET TWO
(CONT.)

WHAT WE
ARE GOING
TO DO

SET A DATE
TO DO
WORKSHEET
THREE
– WHERE WE
ARE NOW

WORKSHEET THREE
WHERE WE ARE NOW

NAME	
DATE	
WHAT ARE MY THOUGHTS NOW?	
HOW DO I FEEL NOW?	
EMOTIONS & FEELINGS	
RATING	

WORKSHEET THREE
(CONT.)

HOW
MUCH THE
EVENT
HAS BEEN
RESOLVED?

IS THERE
ANY
FURTHER
ACTION
REQUIRED?

Appendix V

These are the exercises we talk about in *Chapter Four –
Understanding your filters, prickly thoughts and negative emotions*
and *Chapter Six – Life practicalities*. We have included a blank
exercise form opposite and on the following pages the entire set
of exercises for you to use as a quick reference. Alternatively to
download a complete set of exercise forms ready for use then
please go to **www.oxdev.co.uk**

If you have not yet worked your way through the exercises, we
hope you will take this opportunity here to do so. The exercise
forms include some space for you to write some notes. Feel free
to write down whatever comes to mind. Try not to censor yourself
– there is no right or wrong 'answer'! Please remember that you
are writing to help yourself, your partner and your relationship.

Detailed explanations for Exercises One through Eight are found
in *Chapter Four – Understanding your filters, prickly thoughts
and negative emotions*. For further information on Exercises Nine
through 12, please refer to *Chapter Six – Life practicalities*.

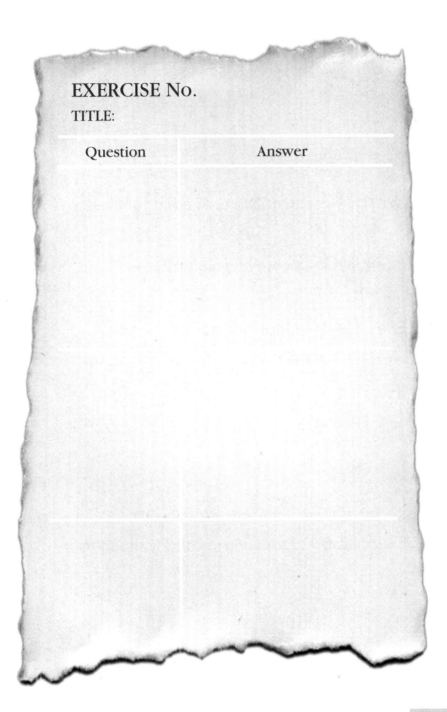

EXERCISE No.

TITLE:

Question	Answer

Exercise 1 – Identifying the strengths

My strengths:

My partner's strengths:

Our strengths as a couple:

Exercise 2 – Identifying our opportunities

Exercise 3 – Identifying our obstacles

Exercise 4 – Prioritizing our list

Exercise 5 – Identifying our filters and beliefs

What I believe about myself:

What I believe about my partner:

What I believe about our relationship:

Exercise 6 – Identifying my prickly thoughts

Prickly thoughts I have about myself:

Prickly thoughts I have about my partner:

Prickly thoughts I have about our relationship:

Exercise 7 – Identifying my negative emotions

Exercise 8 – Identifying what I am getting out of my filters and prickly thoughts

What are the advantages or disadvantages of thinking through your filters and prickly thoughts:

Exercise 9 – Exploring our life practicalities

Exercise 10 – Establishing our aims

My aims:

Our shared aims:

Exercise 11 – Setting our goals

Exercise 12 – Writing our action plan

Acknowledgements

Sadhana Damani

My thanks and appreciation go to my many mentors and colleagues who have taught and inspired me over the years. In particular, I am grateful to Mr. Rod Holland, Mr. Mike O'Neill, Dr. Afreen Huq, Liz Bennett, Ann Richardson and Bridget McCarthy for their confidence in my clinical work. I also thank Dr. Bob Palmer and Dr. Eric Button for their guidance in publishing my work and Dr. Padmal De Silva and Dr. Michael Crowe who encouraged me to write.

My special thanks to my parents who taught me values and to believe in myself. I am grateful for the warmth, support and understanding I received from my husband who inspired me to write this book, as well as, my two loving children. I also thank my family and my friends, especially my friend Larissa Clay for her help in writing this book.

I thank all those who referred their clients to me and, of course, a very special thanks to all of my clients, who in their search for happiness chose to honour me with their trust.

Larissa Clay

My thanks and acknowledgement go out to my family, friends, teachers and colleagues who have given me such valuable support and advice over the years. My special thanks to Sadhana Damani for this collaboration.

My heartfelt thanks to my husband for his patience and unconditional love and support throughout this project and everyday of our lives.

Sadhana Damani & Larissa Clay

Finally, our very special thanks to Dr. Claudia Herbert for her guidance, patient editing and invaluable feedback on the various stages of our manuscript, who made this book a reality.